THE
Ultimate
Guide TO
Shamanism

Inspiring | Educating | Creating | Entertaining

Brimming with creative inspiration, how-to projects, and useful information to enrich your everyday life, Quarto Knows is a favorite destination for those pursuing their interests and passions. Visit our site and dig deeper with our books into your area of interest: Quarto Creates, Quarto Cooks, Quarto Homes, Quarto Lives, Quarto Drives, Quarto Explores, Quarto Gifts, or Quarto Kids.

First Published in 2021 by Fair Winds Press, an imprint of The Quarto Group, 100 Cummings Center, Suite 265-D, Beverly, MA 01915, USA.
T (978) 282-9590 F (978) 283-2742 QuartoKnows.com

Fair Winds Press titles are also available at discount for retail, wholesale, promotional, and bulk purchase. For details, contact the Special Sales Manager by email at specialsales@quarto.com or by mail at The Quarto Group, Attn: Special Sales Manager, 100 Cummings Center, Suite 265-D, Beverly, MA 01915, USA.

25 24 23 22 21   1 2 3 4 5

ISBN: 978-1-59233-996-9

Digital edition published in 2021
eISBN: 978-1-63159-999-6

Library of Congress Cataloging-in-Publication Data

Names: Keating, Rebecca, author.
Title: The ultimate guide to shamanism : a modern guide to shamanic healing, tools, and ceremony / Rebecca Keating.
Description: Beverly, MA, USA : Fair Winds Press, an imprint of The Quarto Group, 2021. | Includes bibliographical references and index. | Summary: «Written by the Founder of the Shaman Sisters, The Ultimate Guide to Shamanism is a modern guide to the ancient practice of using spirit medicine in practice and ceremony for healing and manifestation»-- Provided by publisher.
Identifiers: LCCN 2020049829 | ISBN 9781592339969 (trade paperback) | ISBN 9781631599996 (ebook)
Subjects: LCSH: Shamanism. | Spiritual healing.
Classification: LCC BF1611 .K165 2021 | DDC 201/.44--dc23
LC record available at https://lccn.loc.gov/2020049829

Design: Kate Frances Design
Cover Illustration: Roberta Orpwood
Page Layout: Kate Frances Design
Photography: Nikolina Zelic except Shutterstock on page 13
Illustration: Roberta Orpwood

Printed in China

The information in this book is for educational purposes only. It is not intended to replace the advice of a physician or medical practitioner. Please see your health-care provider before beginning any new health program.

THE
Ultimate
Guide to
Shamanism

A MODERN GUIDE TO SHAMANIC HEALING, TOOLS, AND CEREMONY

Rebecca Keating BScN
CREATOR OF SHAMAN SISTERS

FAIR WINDS

Contents

Author's Note

When you engage in shamanism, you are aligning with the most potent, ancient, and eternal forces of the cosmos. You begin to connect to your true essence and the unseen world around you. You will experience initiations on your journey, as you peel back the layers and step into your gifts, Higher Self, and fullest expression. Although this is a beginner's book on shamanism, these practices are powerfully transformative and should be practiced with sincere intention.

I considered why I was writing this book many times. As a white identifying woman in this life, I have lived many lifetimes in various roles: I have incarnated in many ethnicities and have been a healer, medicine woman, and shaman in many lives. I used shamanic practices to heal and transcend the timelines of abuse and separation. Through my journey of shamanism, I discovered one of my deepest wounds is fear of connection, and through healing I accessed one of my greatest gifts of uniting community. I know that my healing is your healing and your healing is mine.

The global pandemic and protests over racism and indigenous rights have brought so much to the surface. As I wrote this book, I recognized this was all coming up for humanity to acknowledge, honor, heal, and move forward in right relationship. I realized that part of my purpose in writing was to help bring healing. When we shift ourselves, we shift the world: I believe this wisdom is for everyone and is owned by no one. My prayer is to bring healing and reconciliation to our indigenous family in this lifetime and across all lifetimes. For we are all connected, we are all one, we are all a global community, and we are meant to be united.

In this book I offer you a variety of practices in hopes that you find what best suits you and works for you. When it feels good, it comes from the heart. My prayer is for you to access the wisdom of your soul.

Blessings, Reverence & Love A'HO Rebecca Moonlight Owl

Part I
HISTORY AND PRINCIPLES OF SHAMANISM

01
Origins
and History

Since the dawn of time, the call of the unseen universal spirit has taken hold in our hearts. Shamanism is deeply rooted in the unseen, navigating through both natural and supernatural forces in our planet and the cosmos. It is based on the knowledge that you are part of something bigger than just your five mere senses—that you are constantly engaging with the universal field of energy that you can access and tap into for information, guidance, healing, and personal power.

Connecting with the invisible world is part of all cultures, ethnicities, and languages. And shamanism has shifted and changed over the millennia to serve the needs of the community. Considered one of the oldest healing modalities on Earth, it seeks to connect us to the very source of our creation. The role of a shaman can include being a mystic, healer, doctor, priest/priestess, psychotherapist, counselor, storyteller, and keeper of ancient wisdom. It is an integral piece of the fabric of humanity, stretching across continents—and it is still relevant to our society to this day.

The History of Shamanism

Shamanism is an ancient tradition that spans civilizations, continents, and countries. This practice can be traced as far back as humankind itself. Shamanism has existed for as long as we have existed. Shamanism started among hunter-gatherer societies during the Paleolithic era. There is evidence of early humans creating drawings in caves or using remains

of animal bones for rituals. The ancients believed that all animate and inanimate objects were alive, with their own individual spirit and consciousness. These core ideas continued to endure, even while humankind evolved to more agricultural- and farm-based communities.

Historically, the term *shaman* originated from the herding Tungus-speaking tribe in North Asia. It was used to describe the traditional healers, medicine women, and medicine men of Siberia and Mongolia. It is sourced from the word *šaman* and the verb *ša*, which means "to know." This can be translated as "the one who knows."

Over the course of history, shamans were women and men of various ages, as young as preadolescent and onward. The shamans within the tribe were highly respected and were called upon to provide guidance and healing for individuals and for the community.

From a more Western anthropological perspective, shamanism has expanded to include the ritual use of certain practices within a ceremony. These ceremonies provide a formalized, respectful setting in which to honor and communicate with helping spirits and ancestors. Many of these rituals and practices share common traits among various indigenous tribes across the world.

Shamanic practices can be found in a vast range of geographical regions, including Central America, Central Asia, Mesoamerica, Subarctic North America, Europe, Siberia, Japan, Korea, China, Nepal, Bhutan, Egypt, Tibet, and Indonesia. Shamanism also exists in certain indigenous cultures of Australia and Africa.

Each culture created its own unique system, based upon their understanding of the natural world around them and how their ancestors kept and preserved ancient knowledge. Many of these traditions had no written record and were mainly passed on orally from one generation to another. Many indigenous healers do not call themselves shamans. Rather they have terms unique to their own culture, such as *curandero* (Central and South America), *paqo* (Peru), *naguals* (Mexico), *kahuna* (Hawaii), *angakok* (Inuit), or *manang* (Borneo).

Over the centuries, many governments and organized religions have attempted to eliminate, suppress, or vilify the use of shamanism—but it has endured. This may be because at its core, shamanism is deeply grounded in the world and within us.

What Is Shamanism?

Shamanism holds that everything in the universe is interconnected, like a web or fine tapestry. Any feeling of separation is merely an illusion. This allows you to live with an open heart and to know you are connected to everything that is sacred.

Shamanism recognizes that you are a spirit inhabiting a physical body. You are here to learn, grow, and expand. You have experienced many realities, dimensions, and lifetimes, each providing you with what your soul needs for its growth and evolution. Most of humanity has been born into life forgetting this. Shamanism will guide you to heal the wounds and traumas of the past, to remember your gifts and the true nature of who you are.

Shamans are important figures in the community. A shaman may perform ceremonies on behalf of the collective to welcome births into the world and bless marriages and partnerships. In many cultures, key milestones in a person's life, such as the passage from adolescence to adulthood, are celebrated in rituals as rites of passage. Shamans also serve in end-of-life care to listen and hold space for the dying. They guide them to be at peace with anything unresolved in their life. They assist their transition from the physical body and escort the dead consciously, as their souls cross over to the other side. Shamans also offer support to those who have lost a loved one and help them find comfort and mourn in peace. Other key functions a shaman performs are space clearing and offering protection of land and homes. Shamans also use divination to predict future events and weather.

Shamanism is not a religious practice and possesses no dogma. It is a way of life and accessible to everyone, regardless of race, economic status, or culture. There are no rules to follow, no texts to be memorized or repeated, and no deity to worship. Instead, it is grounded in practical, personal experience. This path is rooted deeply in the natural world, centered on direct revelation.

Shamans are not put on display to perform rituals, while the rest of us passively watch. Their work teaches us how to be engaged with the universal forces all around us, both the seen and the unseen, so we can be empowered in our own life. Shamans strive to be a living example of the sacred interaction and reciprocity between humans, the natural world, and the spirit world.

Shamanism as Personal Power

We are always seeking to discover and learn more about ourselves. The practice of shamanism allows you to access your true inner nature—what is true and right for you—and with that connection you will find your own personal power. Power in the shamanic sense is the energy or skill you have to direct the universal energies toward a higher good. Personal power is sacred, and it not about manipulation or control. It is the deepest part of yourself that possesses no attachments, no titles, and no outward achievements to prove status.

This power is also based on reciprocity. A shaman's ability to navigate and influence the unseen forces of the cosmos relies on maintaining balance and integrity in everything he or she does. It is a code of conduct that displays one's reverence and respect. Nature responds. For example, if there is reciprocity, a community's needs will be provided for: there will be enough food, shelter, and clean water for all its people. When things are out of balance, a tribe may experience natural disasters, lack of food or water, or conflict. Ultimately the gifts we receive from both the visible and invisible worlds around us are a direct expression and result of the way we honor this personal power.

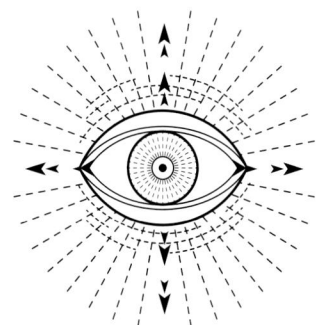

The Difference Between a Shaman and a Shamanic Practitioner

A shaman is typically someone chosen or denoted by the community to heal and lead them. They have demonstrated the appropriate skill and have completed the training and initiation required under a master shaman. This sometimes requires years or decades of practice, depending on the specific cultural customs and traditions.

There are several ways that a traditional shaman can be chosen:

» Through lineage: past ancestors have performed this role.

» Through a traumatic experience, such as being struck by lightning or surviving a serious illness.

» Through an intense initiation practice as outlined by the tribe.

» By demonstrating personal talent or skill.

A shamanic practitioner is someone who engages in shamanic rituals, but might not have been conferred upon by the community to carry out the role of shaman. A practitioner may also have received formal training in a specific tradition or initiation through their ancestors and helping spirits. It is appropriate and acceptable to ask a shamanic practitioner from whom, what, and where they have received training. Out of respect, some shamanic practitioners choose not to call themselves shamans.

SHAMANIC INITIATION

In shamanism, an initiation is when we go through an experience that brings us out of our comfort zone and into an unknown realm. It is the process of shaking up our reality, ripping apart our beliefs, and then putting them back together again anew. Initiation causes us to spiritually die to our old ways of being in the world in order to experience a rebirth through total transformation.

Initiation can come in the form of some of the most challenging events that we've ever had to face. Those challenges are amplified by our resistance: the more we cling to our old ways of being, the more we resist change, the harder it becomes to see the light through the shade.

When we are going through a painful experience, the end result is never known. This can make it very difficult to surrender to and trust in the process. In the midst of suffering and trauma, though, we have to learn to be with what is: to sit with the discomfort, feel whatever emotions arise, and let them pass through us.

Initiation is a catalyst for us to go deep within, into the parts of ourselves that have been repressed so that we can cleanse and release them. Through initiation, we become deeply connected to ourselves, our spirit, and our inner guidance. This connection gives way to a strength that most of us don't even know we have: the strength to withstand the unimaginable, which brings us the gift of soul growth. Trust, surrender, and being able to look at events from another perspective are keys to the process of initiation.

Bridging Ancient Wisdom with Modern Times

The ancient shamans knew that to understand the mysteries of the universe, they had to be intimately connected to nature. Many of their age-old traditions wove the natural world into their rituals. They performed ceremonies of gratitude to their land for providing food and medicine. They sang songs, danced by the fire under the moonlight, adorned their heads and homes with flowers or stones—all to celebrate and honor the great wisdom of Gaia.

Today our connection to ancient knowledge and Mother Earth has been severed. We have isolated ourselves from nature, living in cities with small green spaces and polluted air. In the West, we have further separated ourselves by treating the body, the mind, and the spirit as separate entities. We focus on symptom management, rather than treating the root cause. We feel the strain and emptiness of having to do more and more. We feel the pressure to keep up with technological advances and globalization. And yet, the faster modern life seems to progress, the more we feel the need to connect—because we know something is missing.

Shamanism has survived for so long because it naturally shifts over time with the needs of the people. Its wisdom is timeless and fluid. Many people feel drawn to it because at its core it is the study of our inner selves and our connection to our environment. Shamanism aims to help us develop our human consciousness to achieve harmony between ourselves and the natural world.

The shaman activates the inner knowing that allows our true, limitless nature to be explored and enhanced. Part of why shamanism is experiencing a renaissance is because we realize this is essential: we want to understand ourselves better, feel connected to others, and find a sense of purpose. We have an inner knowing there is more. These ancient practices can guide you toward a deeper wisdom. They can support you in facing the challenges of modern life and help reestablish your relationship with Mother Earth and your Higher Self.

Evolving with the Times

Today many shamanic practices use the tools, language, symbols, and metaphors that are familiar and accessible to us in the modern world. For example, many indigenous cultures for thousands of years have believed that we come from the stars. Now, astrophysics confirms it. All that has changed is our scientific language. We can better understand concepts that shamans have known for thousands of years by using our modern scientific framework to explain it.

We may not perform ceremonies by a mountaintop or beside the raging sea, and we may not host large bonfires with our entire tribe. Yet we can still deeply experience shamanism for ourselves. We can create a sacred altar in our home dedicated to our spiritual practice. We can light a candle to transform our energy or pay respect to an ancestor. We can pay homage to Mother Earth by carrying a small stone or crystal found in our backyard or when we visit a pond or stream near our city. These are moments when we can truly engage.

By adopting and shifting our rituals and tools, we can bring forth the ancient practice of shamanism into this modern world. Even if you live in a concrete jungle and can find no evidence of nature, you can still go within and journey to nature. The inner shaman lives inside of you.

How to Use This Book

This book is a guide for you to bring traditional and modern shamanic practices into your everyday life. It will not teach you to become a shaman, but it will provide the tools and methods to help you access your own inner spirit and wisdom for self-development, growth, and healing so that you can experience life in its fullest expression. This will allow you to find and utilize your true gifts. When you access the source of knowledge inside your Higher Self, you can discover your life's purpose and reach higher levels of consciousness or even attain enlightenment.

We are waking up to these long-forgotten practices. We can bridge the knowledge of science with the spirit of the sacred. Something inside and within you yearns to connect to the deepest part of your history and humanity. For those who heed the calling, shamanism is a way of life.

In this book you will find practical and modern exercises that incorporate precious tools from the world around you—crystals, herbs, stones, essential oils, and flowers. You can do most of these rituals, ceremonies, and meditations in your own home or out in nature. Read through the easy-to-follow instructions and incorporate them at your own pace. Remember that the key component of shamanism is your own intention and your energy.

Ultimately this is about your own personal journey to connect with your spirit, the unseen worlds and to find the shaman within. This book can help you access those nonordinary states and those spiritual realms. The universal life force energy is accessible to you, not just the chosen few. With dedicated practice and an open heart, you will begin to live the shamanic principles in your everyday life.

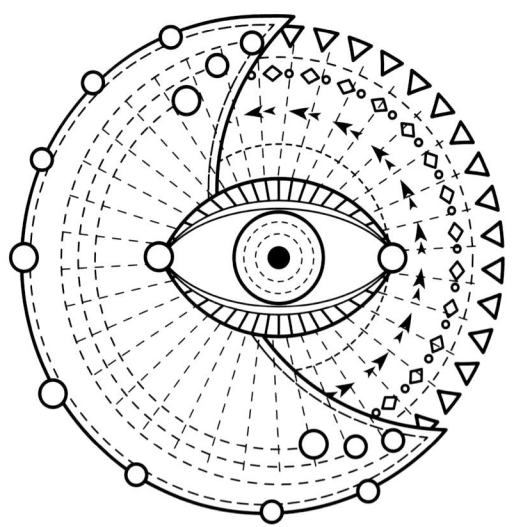

02
Shamanism of the Modern Day

The nostalgic image of a shaman as a primitive, isolated person with mysterious powers, living hidden away in the forest, is a thing of the past. Today's shaman still uses ancient wisdom to harness great change within an individual or a community, but the methods and the context have changed. The core function of a shaman is engagement and direct interaction in order to harness change, and our view of a shaman is evolving to keep pace with modern expectations.

Traditionally a shaman would dress in full regalia, colorful robes, or elaborate headdresses and feathers. Nowadays these carriers of the ancient traditions are usually dressed plainly. In their everyday life, shamans look very much like the rest of us. Shamanism has also adapted to be more accessible to contemporary urbanites and city dwellers. These shifts allow shamanism to continue to be relevant within the current social, economic, and cultural environment. If the shaman's primary role is to serve the community, then they must go to where the people are.

Depending on the practitioner, shamanism may or may not be linked to a specific cultural- or lineage-based practice. Shamans typically use the most efficient and practical methods that have stood the test of time. You may also see a blending of traditions or practices to suit modern culture or a particular group. For example, the Hindu chakra system may be referenced alongside many other traditions or ceremonies.

The role of the modern shaman is to find truths from within ourselves. We receive these truths from our Higher Self, through our own guidance and intuition. We can turn to our elders to guide us in remembering who we truly are and how to once again connect with Mother Nature. While our fast-paced world can sometimes leave us confused and overwhelmed, our indigenous ancestors remind us how to connect with the Universal Source directly. Ultimately this wisdom is innate within us all, and while a shaman may assist us by leading the way, our individual shamanic expression is unique, like a work of art. We learn to cocreate a harmonious life and world. Modern shamanism has a place for all of us.

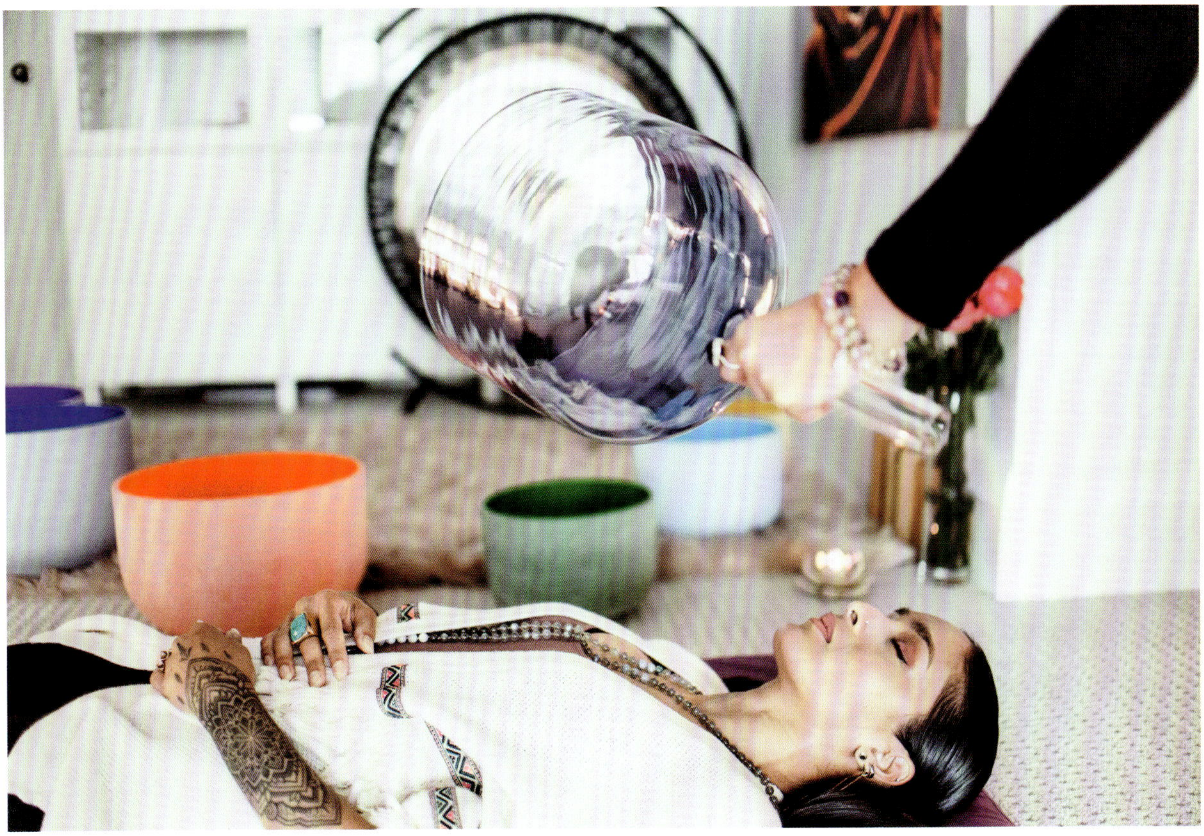

The Benefits of Living a Shamanic Lifestyle

At the heart of shamanism is the understanding that we are all one. We are an integral part of an intelligent universe, both seen and unseen. This principle allows us to feel a greater sense of purpose. We are not separate from Mother Nature—she needs us as much as we need her. When we understand this, we know that we are not alone.

Integrating shamanic principles into your everyday life can bring you more peace and centeredness. In the modern age, where anxiety and depression are prevalent, stepping into your vitality and personal power can positively affect your health: the immune system improves, addictions are released, and your connection to the Universal Source is strengthened. Even your relationships with your family, spouse, loved ones, and friends can benefit. When you see everything as sacred, you carry yourself and your relationships in a different way. There is no separation between anything that exists in nature. It is a powerful realization of oneness and integration.

The shamanic lifestyle is an empowering one. Shamanism teaches you to connect to yourself as the innermost spiritual authority. You do not require an intermediary or authority figure to "decode," approve, or grant messages from the Divine to you. Living a shamanic lifestyle means you choose to take back the power yourself, when you realize that you have an inherent capability to connect to universal divine wisdom. You do not need to look outside of yourself for spiritual guidance or enlightenment. We no longer choose to bypass our own internal knowing and higher wisdom to someone else. We are all special, and we are all worthy—this is our birthright.

A shamanic lifestyle helps you build trust and faith in your own abilities and gifts. As you engage in regular and daily practices to connect to the many sources of energy around us, you know and understand that you were created by a vast intelligence that loves you. You begin to take firmer steps into your highest destiny and purpose, because you know you are supported by the cosmic intelligences and by your Higher Self, which is the eternal aspect of you—the intelligence that is always with you.

Neoshamanism and Cultural Appropriation

The concept of neoshamanism emerged out of the need to experience cross-cultural awakening and awareness, focused on individual enlightenment and well-being. It was a term born from the rebellious antiestablishment movements of the 1960s and 1970s, seeking new methods to solve the world's societal and environmental problems. Neo, from the Greek word *néos*, means "new," describing the new form of multidisciplinary shamanic practices.

Neoshamanism was driven in part by a desire to take control of one own's health and healing, while reestablishing a respect and reverence for nature. It was an attempt to experience shamanism for oneself, rather than from a textbook or a limited Western anthropological perspective. These experiences include everything from traveling to "non-ordinary" reality, moments of ecstasy, achieving altered states, or acting as a facilitator between the earthly plane and the spirit world.

This practice of combining and adapting traditions, especially from indigenous origins, can be seen as cultural appropriation. Colonization has done irreparable damage to many indigenous groups across the globe. In an attempt to forge new creations for a global age, neoshamanism can appear to strip indigenous groups of their unique cultural markers, essentially assimilating or "watering down" the true origins of their craft.

No one culture in existence today can definitively say it is the ultimate source of shamanism. The wisdom in these traditions carries resonance

throughout the world on every continent. Because of this, we see shamanism as an inclusive practice that honors and respects many traditions. The basic tenet of shamanism is one of wholeness and holding every piece of this Earth, including ourselves as humans, as valuable and sacred. Shamanism belongs to everyone. The call of the great Universal Source also belongs to each of us.

We recognize and acknowledge the wounding and the abuse that has taken place in centuries past. The intergenerational trauma that was created continues to reverberate through Indigenous people today. And while we cannot change the past, we can stand against systematic racism and disconnection from one another in the present. United we can contribute to the global spread of these much needed teachings. As humankind grows in our consciousness and ascends beyond our three-dimensional body and senses, we seek a return to oneness with all sentient beings. Together we must strive to keep these ancient teachings alive, preserve them with respect, and share them with others when appropriate. After all, it is from these core shamanic principles and ideas that our species has survived for thousands of years.

Shamanism provides the keys to purifying separation consciousness and our collective wounds and traumas. Humanity is awakening to the illusion of separation and egoistic constructs. The truth of unity consciousness comes alive through the power of our hearts. Keeping shamanism secret or coveted from certain groups only creates further division. The Indigenous people around the world are the keepers of these ancient teachings and despite numerous groups being stripped of their culture and rights, many have generously share their wisdom and we must honor and respect them.

As we learn to heal ourselves by walking the shamanic path, we also learn to heal our lineage. Humanity needs these universal teachings, as they hold keys to transcending into the next stage of our evolution, both as individuals and as a collective. Shamanism is meant to be accessible to all. Our work on the shamanic path is to sow unity, not discord. Everything we do in shamanism seeks to bring us together. It is only by doing so that we can truly live in harmony with ourselves and Mother Earth, as we were always meant to do.

Shamanism is a core practice of wholeness, unity, and sanctity. Everyone and everything is included— every human, rock, tree, insect, plant, bird, animal, grain of sand . . . the formless wind we can still feel on our faces and the hardened concrete structures around us. We pay homage to all of it. You are invited to be a part of it and experience the return of wholeness for yourself.

Finding the
Shaman Within

Healing on physical, emotional, mental, and spiritual levels can be achieved by looking inward: slow down, find a quiet place, connect to your breath, and open your heart to the universe. This allows your nervous system to calm down. Then you can get back in touch with yourself and not separate yourself from your body, mind, and spirit.

We can access the healer within when we surrender and become a witnessing observer. Look to nature to see how effortlessly things are accomplished. For example, the oak tree continues to grow taller over time, with little strife or exertion. When we surrender and slow down, we can learn to listen and engage with the invisible spirits all around us. In this way, we can access our Higher Selves and the wisdom of the ancestors and receive the messages they give us. True healing always comes from the inside.

Both our physical bodies and our minds are perfect vehicles to help us reach a state of balance and optimal health. The body is wise; it is always searching for homeostasis—the body naturally wants to heal itself. Our job is to remove any blocks that prevent this natural process from occurring on its own. We do this by connecting to, appreciating, and grounding our bodies.

Often we focus on our pain or what's not working with our bodies and we feel the urge to fight. Instead we should look upon our body as the miracle it is—every ache, every pain, teaches us to listen and connect more deeply to ourselves. These pains are signs to get our attention. For example, our navel area and our womb store an enormous ability to perceive, evaluate, and conduct energy. When we speak of a "gut instinct," this is a real phenomenon. Listening to what our gut or womb region is telling us is often a clue about how we should process a particular person or situation. As they say, the gut never lies. The key is for us to learn to trust and reclaim this inborn ability within us.

Your Connection to Yourself

Many practices, such as yoga and qi gong, teach us how to reconnect through physical movement with the Earth, by using simple, time-tested movements. The ceremonies and rituals in this book, such as grounding to the Earth element or making a simple bath with beautiful ingredients, will also allow you to reconnect to your body.

Our brain also has a vast capacity to heal itself through images, symbols, and repetition. That is why meditation and mantras are so effective. Auto-suggestions or mantras (short, repetitive phrases) are a simple way of introducing and injecting desired thoughts and ideas from our conscious mind to our subconscious mind. We are essentially reprogramming the neural pathways in our brain to create a new story, a new outcome, and a new result. We learn to quiet the "monkey mind," the ego thoughts that attempt to question and make meaning out of every circumstance or conversation. When we recognize our pain and the beliefs associated with it, we can heal ourselves emotionally. Using mantras or repetitive affirmations to positively influence your brain can also help you better achieve your goals and fulfill your dreams.

Mantras and Self-Healing Affirmations

» FOR SELF-LOVE: I love and accept myself unconditionally.

» FOR HEALTH: My body is wise. I am in perfect health. I am balanced physically, emotionally, and mentally. I love and respect my body.

» FOR ABUNDANCE: I gratefully and easily attract abundance and wealth in all forms.

» FOR CONFIDENCE: I trust myself and my abilities. I am excellent at everything I do.

» FOR SPIRITUALITY: I connect easily with the great, Universal Source. I am one with the Creator.

» FOR A LIFE PARTNER: I am whole and confident in myself. I consciously choose to attract a life partner who complements, respects, and supports me.

» FOR LIFE PURPOSE: Every day I am living my life's purpose. The work I do fills me with great joy. I make a difference in the world. My work is my highest calling.

» FOR CREATIVITY: I easily tap into the creative flow. I have many excellent ideas.

» FOR BODY IMAGE: I am beautiful. I unconditionally love and accept my body, my shape, my skin. I am exactly as my Creator intended. There are no flaws in the Creator's design.

03
Shamanic
Principles

For shamans, everything is alive and everything has a vibration. We use ceremonies and rituals to tap into the universal unseen energy field. Our five senses serve us in many necessary ways, yet they are also very limited in their abilities. This is especially true when it comes to our perception of time and the space-time continuum. Because we exist in linear time, we tend to think of past lives and reincarnation as occurring in another distant time of the past. Every lifetime we have ever had is occurring now. Everything past, present, and future is occurring simultaneously.

Shamans can work in our unseen lives and help us find healing. Tapping into the support and wisdom of your ancestors, also known as ancestral medicine or ancestral healing, can also restore your sense of wholeness and personal power.

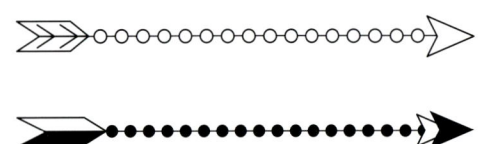

Respecting and Honoring Sacred Traditions

Shamanism and its practices should be treated with reverence and respect. The wisdom passed down to us from our elders and ancestors of previous generations is valuable and sacred. We are merely accessing their past knowledge and wisdom to help the collective. It would be extreme hubris to believe that we are the source of shamanic wisdom; therefore, paying homage to the ancestors is a core shamanic principle.

Various ways shamans honor their ancestors are by:

» Singing or drumming specific music or songs

» Telling stories or "myths" about ancestors and legendary experiences

» Dancing in a circle or by the fire

» Creating an ancestral altar and offering the finest food, sweets, snacks, or drinks

» Framing photos or images of the elders and putting them in a prominent place

» Burning or burying sacred offerings such as incense, tobacco, essential oils, flowers, herbs, textiles, precious metals, or stones

Most shamanic traditions have cultural markers, customs, symbols, and language that make them distinct from others. Learn how to balance both the unique qualities of a specific lineage and tradition while still blending it effectively with modern-day needs. The best way to imagine this is through the symbol of a braid—although we recognize each strand within the braid to be unique on its own, we can also learn to blend each strand together to form a beautiful pattern. This method allows respectful integration, while still valuing the individuality of each strand on its own.

For example, some shamanic teachers, despite having been trained in multiple traditions (such as the Native North American versus Celtic or Andean shamanic traditions), may keep the knowledge and practices separate from each lineage, rather than combining them. The choice is up to the individual shaman or practitioner, depending on the situation and what feels right in their heart and often what they have been given permission to do. The most important factor to consider is always your intention. No matter what you are practicing, you must always consciously be aware of what you are doing and know why you are doing it. As long as you imbue each practice with the utmost love and respect, you can be sure you are acting in highest alignment and integrity.

Ceremony and Ritual

A ceremony is defined as a structured gathering of people for a specific purpose, with specific customs and practices attached to them. They can be religious or cultural. They can be elaborate practices or very simple. A ceremony may be performed by an individual, a family (clan/tribe), the community, or even a nation. Over time, these specific customs get passed on from family to family, from generation to generation. Although it may seem "old-fashioned" to talk about ancient ceremonies such as drum circles or fire dances, we have kept many of these similar practices in modern times. Any time we celebrate a marriage, attend a graduation, or honor a loved one at a funeral, we are participating in a ceremony.

Shamanic ceremonies can be performed during life changes, rites of passages, or the changing of seasons. They are also used to bring blessings or clear unwanted energy from a person or space. During times of transition, engaging in ceremony helps us be less resistant to change, by honoring the natural cycles of life. When we release what needs to be let go instead of holding on to it, we can make space for something new to arise. By stating our intentions and calling in the assistance of helping spirits and

ancestors in a focused way, we can become cocreators of our reality. Through the practice of ceremony, we bring flow and ease into our lives and we bring healing to ourselves and to the community.

A ceremony is typically more formal and performed occasionally, whereas a ritual is an exercise, a practice, or a behavior that may or may not have a special meaning attached to it. Rituals are usually performed regularly—for example, a daily meditation practice is a ritual. However, in the shamanic sense, everything we do should be infused with intent.

Today's ceremonies and rituals may look quite different from ancient versions, but the purpose remains the same. The ancestors knew that these weren't merely performances for show; they were important signals of respect and reciprocity to Mother Nature and the cosmos. They are an earnest and steadfast exchange of our highest energies. When we offer our gifts to Mother Earth and Father Sky, and the Creator in this humble way, we are often rewarded many times over. For example, the Andean Despacho is a sacred ritual outlined on page 156 of this book.

Past Lives and Reincarnation

Have you ever found yourself fascinated or attracted to certain countries, sacred sites, or places you've never been? Do you resonate with past civilizations? Do you experience déjà vu, or an uncanny feeling that you've been somewhere before? As a new situation unfolds, does it seem familiar somehow?

Unexplained fears or phobias can be other indications of a past life. For example, a person may have a fear of water, even though they have never experienced a drowning incident before, or a phobia of spiders, even though they have never been bitten. On the opposite end of the spectrum, you may possess physical or intellectual skills that go beyond the average performance level yet come easily to you. These could all be clues to occurrences in other lifetimes.

In the shamanic view and in many spiritual traditions, our soul existence is not linear and does not start and end with birth and death. The soul continues on and fulfills the lessons, sometimes painful ones, that it needs to learn along the way. Many of these unexplained experiences can be residual traces of a simultaneous life, in a different body, on a different timeline. A past life or simultaneous life shows that our essence is the soul—not just our physical body. Our soul needs to undergo various circumstances to learn and grow. Thus, we are constantly born and reborn into new bodies and new lifetimes to experience, evolve, and achieve our highest purpose. When we understand our true essence as a soul, we are truly immortal. Our bodies are merely the outer "packaging" we choose to traverse in this lifetime.

Reincarnation is the process whereby we leave our physical bodies in one lifetime and then choose to "reappear" in another body, in another lifetime, to learn more lessons. It is a conscious continuity of the soul for rebirth in simultaneous existences. For example, the current Dalai Lama, Tenzin Gyatso, is considered to be the fourteenth reincarnation of the patron saint of Tibet, the Bodhisattva of Compassion.

Reincarnation refers to the soul continuing on after death. We experience linear time in the 3rd dimension. In linear time, other lifetimes are referred to as past lives as they appear to be occurring in the past.

In reality, we are multidimensional and exist in other planes simultaneously—time is not linear.

Everything past, present, and future is occurring at the same time in different realities or frequencies. From a shamanic perspective, death is nothing to fear because our soul and Higher Self are eternal.

All energy is never created or destroyed; it is simply transformed or changed from one form into another. Since Mother Earth shows us how easily She can recycle energy in nature, why would humans be any different?

Because we have experienced many lifetimes on many planes, in many cultures, and in many time periods, our soul and our bodies have also experienced traumas—there is no escaping it. Shamans understand that healing may also need to come from this much deeper level—to recover and reclaim the wounds inflicted in our simultaneous lifetimes. Many of these traumas are stored in our subconscious, which can explain certain habits or tendencies, such as irrational phobias or inexplicable behavioral patterns. These are wounds that have yet to be resolved or healed fully. Eventually our soul will move on from the cycle of reincarnation and onto other experiences.

When a shaman is working within the unseen world of another lifetime, he or she is looking for those unclaimed soul parts that require recognition and healing. Gaining an understanding into our unseen lives can be one of the best ways to liberate ourselves from negative patterns and repetitive wounds. Soul retrieval can be used to heal past-life traumas.

Healing the Lineage

Some say that when we begin our shamanic journey to healing, we are also healing seven generations before us and seven generations after us. It is an extremely powerful notion to understand that you are not just healing yourself and your simultaneous lifetimes, but also your ancestral line and the future generations to come.

If our lives are a link inside a long chain of ancestral beliefs, thoughts, actions, and consequences, then we can see how it may have affected our current life situation. Many of us carry the burden subconsciously of previous generations of oppression, silence, colonialism, even genocide, plus familial or tribal covenants or curses, painful addictions, tendency toward anger or violence, old enemies, grievances or feuds, and limiting beliefs. Imagine yourself as the brave person who is breaking the chain. When you do this, the entire ancestral lineage has the potential to evolve and heal.

In many cultures, it is customary to hold festivals and rituals to honor the ancestors who have passed on, such as Mexico's Día de los Muertos or Day of the Dead; in China, it is customary to have ancestral shrines with regular offerings. Our Western culture has tended to view these activities as superstitious, until the emerging fields of epigenetics, cellular biology, and neurobiology are proving that at least three generations of family history should be examined when studying the mechanisms and patterns of trauma within an individual. This is no longer the arena of "superstition," but the realm of science.

When scientists began mapping the human genome, it was believed that our genes determined our destiny. However, as research progressed, scientists uncovered that only 2 percent of our chromosomal DNA (which determines our physical attributes such as our height, hair, skin color, or eye color) makes up our total DNA. The other 98 percent is known as noncoding or "junk DNA," which influences how DNA is transcribed into proteins, ensuring the chromosomal bundles form properly within the cell's nucleus for its survival. The "junk DNA" portion also affects our personality, behavioral patterns, and emotional traits. This inactive DNA is not really "junk" as it holds our highest potential and is activated as our frequency raises.

Now, with the emerging field of epigenetics, we are beginning to understand how traits, traumas, and information can be passed on from one generation to the next, without appearing to alter the DNA. Our cells have learned to express themselves in other ways, aside from merely the chromosomes of our DNA—our cells can turn the gene expression "on" or "off," through chemical tags. The cells have literally adapted to determine whether a gene should or should not be expressed.

This becomes important because epigenetics can explain how other variables, outside of straight genetic sequencing, such as emotional stressors, environmental factors, and trauma, can be passed on from generation to generation. We are products of both nature and nurture. This emerging field of science shows us how our cells express themselves differently, influenced by various lifestyle and environmental factors. The inheritance of generational trauma is a real phenomenon that can now be supported by science.

One way we can repair and honor our lineage is by sharing and preserving the ancient ways. For centuries, many indigenous, holistic, or spiritual groups that did not comply with the dominant religious force were often condemned and suppressed. Now, with a new age of consciousness dawning before us, it is a great privilege to bring these teachings and ancient wisdoms forward. No longer will we be told what spiritual practices to have and how we can connect to the spirit. Most important, when you learn of the ancestors' healing gifts, you know that you are not alone and are always supported.

Ancestral Healing Exercise

This exercise will help you tap into the wisdom of your ancestors and heal the legacy of any wounds that no longer serve your highest good.

Begin this exercise by researching the names of

your maternal and paternal grandparents and your biological parents. You'll need their full names and where they were born. If you don't have all of this information, that's okay: you can also state your intention and the energy of calling in your ancestors.

Find a quiet place where you will not be disturbed for at least 20 to 30 minutes.

Place an altar cloth with a few special items in front of you. If you already have an altar set up (see page 68), you may use this sacred altar instead. You may choose to place photos on your altar.

Light a candle or several candles. Burn herbs or incense and add fresh flowers to bring beauty into the space.

Begin to bring attention to your breath. Close your eyes. Begin to relax your body, as you continue to breathe deeply.

Intend only for the benevolent ancestors and those who wish to hold you in the highest good in unconditional love to be present. Now envision your immediate family members in a circle, holding hands. Visualize your maternal grandparents standing behind your mother figure and your paternal grandparents standing behind your father figure. You may also choose to expand to your great-grandparents, if you wish.

Feel the support of your grandparents standing behind your parents and your family. Envision this entire group circle being held in a golden light. Your entire family lineage is being enveloped and sustained by a large, yellow circle of pure light.

Thank your ancestors for being present and for sharing the wisdom and the lessons they have learned on their life's path. Tell them you are willing to release any old negative beliefs and patterns held in your ancestry. You wish to move forward in forgiveness and unconditional love. Show your

gratitude for your ancestors' lives and the sacrifices they have made. You acknowledge and revere all they have done to bring you into this life.

Intend that any ancestral energies that no longer serve your highest good be fed into the candle's fire. You may symbolically hold both cupped palms as the container for the old energies that now need to be released. Place both hands over the candle, as you symbolically pour these energies into the fire to be transformed. Give thanks and love for this process.

If it feels right to you, consider offering food or drink to your ancestors as gratitude. This could include water, tea, fruits, or sweet snacks. These offerings can remain at the altar for several days or a week, or until the next auspicious cycle. When this is complete, the offerings may be buried in the earth or burned.

04
Shamanic Energy Medicine

The fundamental understanding of how energy works is an important component to how shamans heal. Through ritual and ceremony, shamans can traverse other dimensions and realities, communicate with spirits, transmute energies, and assist in your healing. Understanding how to work with your own energy is key to healing and self-mastery.

Science tells us that everything is energy. From the blade of grass, to the smooth pebble on the beach, from your physical body, to the stars in the sky—every part of the universe is made up of vibrational energy. Shamans do their healing work at the soul level. Shamanic energy healing interacts with the subtle, unseen energy field, also known in many traditions as the life force or *prana* (an ancient Sanskrit word for breath or "vital principle") or *chi* (a Chinese word for "universal energy flow"). No matter what the term, this is the divine energy of the soul. We are all derived from this vast, universal energetic source.

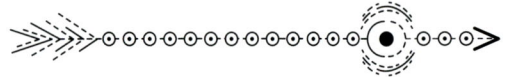

Quantum Physics and Energy

"All matter originates and exists only by virtue of a conscious and intelligent non-visible living energy force. This energy force is the matrix mind of all matter."

—MAX PLANCK, DEVELOPER OF QUANTUM THEORY

For thousands of years, shamans have worked at the level of quanta, the unseen, or the subatomic. Only in recent history has quantum physics begun to explain what shamans have known for millennia.

Atoms are the building blocks of life that create matter. The Newtonian model of matter and the atom (think Styrofoam "balls and sticks") led us to

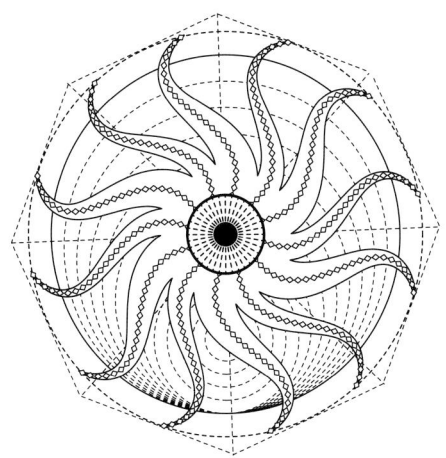

What Does It Mean to Be Conscious?

Sometimes automatic programming can be useful. For example, you don't want to think too much every morning you get up to brush your teeth, get dressed, and drive to work. Our brains have developed neural pathways for our most common movements and routines. You also can appreciate your body's instinctive mechanisms, such as every time you eat an apple: you don't have to instruct your esophagus, throat, or stomach to digest it and extract the nutrients, while discarding the waste—this happens automatically. Science also tells us that 80 percent of our thoughts are just as routine. We just replay the same scenario over and over again from one day to the next, with little change or originality.

Being conscious means you are stepping away from the veil of illusion—you become fully aware of your body's mechanisms, your egoic thoughts, your emotions, and your actions. You are an active participant and a neutral witness to everything that happens in your life. When you are fully conscious, you are fully aware of every moment. This is what we mean when we speak about "presence"—it is about being attentive and responsive to the moment. In that space, there is no past and there is no future, only the present. Once you can learn to tap into this space, you will see reality as it is.

Meditation can help us tap into this state of consciousness. We realize we are not our thoughts or our brain. Once you learn to distance yourself from just the physical body and mind, you also learn to occupy a space that is less tangible, more invisible, yet just as valuable. This is the space where you can

believe that we were primarily made of matter. We believed that the outcomes were predictable and that humans operated within a set of physical laws.

Enter Albert Einstein. His famous equation, $E = MC^2$, essentially proved that energy and matter were relatable and interchangeable. Matter is not separate from energy, and energy is not separate from matter. Because of explorations in quantum physics, we now know that at a subatomic level, the atom is actually 99.99 percent empty space. This means that the solid table sitting in front of you, or the palm of your hand, is built mainly upon empty space. It might seem strange to you that a solid table is actually made up of tiny, invisible packets of subatomic particles you can't see. At the quantum level, things move at the speed of light and our senses cannot perceive the quantum world at this speed.

Atoms are invisible and electrical, operating like tiny batteries. Within the atom there is a positive charge and a negative charge (i.e., protons and electrons). Your physical body is made up of 100 trillion atoms, making you an electrical being. But you are also essentially, mostly empty space. This means that there is opportunity to influence and affect this empty space, also known as your energy field.

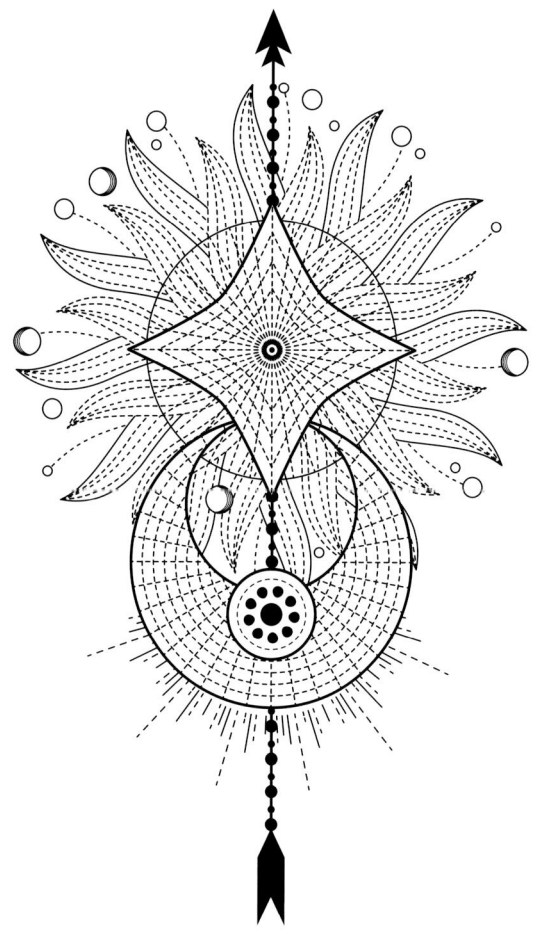

From a deeper shamanic perspective, shamans explore the source of your emotions and feelings. Shamans are not only aware of them, but they also understand how and where they came from, and how to better navigate the realms consciously. From a shaman's viewpoint, when you are conscious and aware, you no longer need to assign blame and guilt to others. You see fear, anger, and shame for what they are: internal wounds and traumas that need to be healed. You step away from being a victim and into self-awareness.

This is a powerful practice, because once you learn that you are in control of your emotions and your actions, you are able to witness them from a neutral perspective. You don't let your emotions run you. You can step into personal accountability and make choices from an aware and empowered place.

The Subconscious Realm

"Until you make the unconscious conscious, it will direct your life and you will call it fate."

—CARL JUNG

access the direct wisdom of your Higher Self and the spirit world.

Being conscious also means you are able to observe your emotions and your feelings. An emotion is defined as a reaction to a person or an event. Emotions can be positive, negative, or somewhere in between. A feeling is a much more curated, intentional response—how you feel about something is usually a sign of your awareness. How does a situation or person make us feel? Instead of reacting immediately with an emotional response, a feeling is a much more conscious effort to use the body or the mind to determine how those feelings should guide us.

The subconscious stores everything that has ever happened to you: your memories in this life and beyond, your skills, and your beliefs. It is also the barrier and filter between what you experience firsthand with your five senses and what your conscious mind can perceive.

Your senses can gather approximately 11 million bits of information per second and send them to your brain, but your conscious mind can process only about 50 to 120 bits per second. Your eyesight has the greatest capability to transmit the highest amount of information to the brain (10,000,000 bits per second), while your sense of taste has the lowest (1,000 bits per second). The subconscious mind acts as a processing mechanism for you to filter out what is most relevant to you in a particular situation and most important, and this helps you survive.

To plumb the mind of the subconscious is where the real work lies. One of the most important functions of a shaman is to examine and bring forth the secrets and the beliefs of the subconscious, to heal ourselves. The work of the shaman is to traverse the realms where our conscious minds cannot decipher the information provided to us. That is why so much of a shaman's work is considered "hidden" or "within the darkness." What they are referring to is the subconscious realm, which gathers and processes information beyond the five senses.

What most of us don't realize is that many components of our subconscious have been programmed either from birth or from early childhood. This is not always intentional, but it often makes us feel "stuck" or trapped in repetitive patterns that can seem out of our control. Having a conscious awareness of this means you can direct your personal power for your highest good. First, you become aware of the program's existence, then you can start to release yourself from it—to make atonements where they are needed and to heal your internal wounds.

Sometimes these subconscious wounds and programs may be sourced from our past lives and ancestors' lives, and are not solely our own. Science has shown that we inherit trauma directly into our DNA for at least three generations. For example, your fear of scarcity, of never having enough, may actually come from your ancestors who lived during wartime or famine. The trauma they experienced lodged itself into their DNA and implanted this pattern into future generations for protection and also harm. To survive the trauma and return to ordinary life, these painful memories were suppressed and retreated into the subconscious. Unfortunately many of these traumas lie "dormant," until they can find a different pathway to express themselves—usually through another family member or another intense disturbance or ordeal brings it to light. When the conscious part of your brain shuts down and cannot process a traumatic event, it may manifest as mental or physical strife in your life.

Another common subconscious wound is the fear of using your healing gifts. For centuries, it was not safe to speak about or practice the healing arts, holistic forms of medicine, or shamanism. Medicine women, indigenous tribes, shamans, and witches were prosecuted and executed en masse, often burned at the stake. Women were forced to turn on each other, to protect themselves and their families. These healers were persecuted for expressing their natural gifts. These memories have been stored in our subconscious, manifesting as blockages, fears, and doubts.

On a conscious level, this type of ancestral wound runs so deeply that it may have prevented many with natural healing abilities today from seeking a career in holistic or energy medicine. Fortunately, it is now more acceptable to discuss spiritual concepts and natural medicines, although many people are still releasing these imprints in our subconsciousness and energetic field. Part of the shaman's work is to retrieve these subconscious memories and bring them into the light. They do this by reading and engaging with your energy field and your soul.

Energy Fields of the Human Body

The Western system of medicine seeks to heal by separating the body from its energetic source. It focuses mainly on identifying and eliminating the pathogen to treat or cure a disease, often with the use of pharmaceuticals, rather than looking at an individual holistically. We separate the person from the environment or other energetic causes that could be the root of the problem.

The shamanic view of wellness understands that your physical, mental, emotional, and spiritual health are deeply interconnected. One of the ways shamans bring the body into balance is by working in the energetic fields. These subtle bodies exist as layers (similar to an onion) comprised of electromagnetic frequencies that extend beyond and interpenetrate with your physical body. Known also as your light body or aura, these energy fields are an extension of your soul, where physical matter intersects with consciousness. The aura connects to the physical body through your energy centers, also known as *chakras* in the Hindu tradition. Other cultures have different names for the energy centers. There are also finer energy channels that distribute energy throughout the physical body, called meridians in the Chinese tradition.

This means you are more than just your physical body. Your aura surrounds your physical form and exists as higher frequencies of vibrating energy (made up of light and sound) that keeps you alive and acts as a protective shield for you. The chakras receive, assimilate, and transmit the energy, distributing it to the physical body, organs, and glands. The meridians supply energy to every part of your body. Many cultures from around the world have integrated this knowledge into their healing systems, from the ancient Chinese (traditional Chinese medicine) to the ancient Indians (Ayurveda).

What the ancients knew is that having a clear, smooth energy flow creates a healthy life. From the cells in the body to the glands, organs, and tissues, these diverse energy systems supply the power that enables the biochemical processes to keep us alive, and they even help inform our DNA. Illness starts in the energy field and then manifests in the physical body. Therefore, if this crucial energy flow is blocked or unbalanced, it can lead to illness and disease. Left unchecked for years or decades, this could lead to terminal illnesses or death.

Once you open your mind and your heart to the understanding that wellness goes beyond just the physical body or the five senses, you begin to understand that everything is energetic and interconnected. Having an awareness and understanding of how to clear, balance, and activate the subtle energy fields of the body is fundamental to your well-being, physical health, and spiritual evolution. When your energy fields are balanced, in harmony and in coherence, it is reflected in all aspects of your life.

The Aura

The word *aura* originates from the Greek and means "breath" or "breeze." In modern times, the word has shifted to mean a distinctive radiance or an energy around a living thing.

Your aura is the subtle electromagnetic energy field that extends around and penetrates your physical body. The aura, also known as the light body, is your first energetic defense system; it filters and protects you from outside energies—it holds the data of all your life experiences across time and space.

This field can be perceived in multiple ways, depending on the individual: it can be seen through colors, felt through vibrations, or just an inner, imperceptible knowing. Your aura is permeable and penetrable, composed of different frequencies and colors, forming a luminous cocoon around you. It is made up of seven layers of subtle energy bodies, each having its own function. The subtle bodies are always sensing and processing information and working together to maintain balance within your body and energy pathways.

When you bring awareness to how your physical body and subtle bodies function together, you will operate at a higher level. For example, your conscious and unconscious thoughts effect your emotional state. When you begin to be self-aware of the mental and emotional bodies by discovering your disempowering thought forms, reactions, and triggers, you can restore harmony and balance to your energy field.

As you clear energies that inhibit you, and when your subtle bodies are not out of balanced or restricted, they will work synergistically together. You will be in tune with yourself on a deeper level and you will have more peace and harmony in your life. Healing and consciously integrating the subtle bodies will allow you to perceive from a pure state, rather than a distorted one. Working on clearing and aligning the subtle bodies will bring you self-awareness and personal power, allowing you to connect with your Higher Self to retrieve your own answers. The latent DNA within you can become activated as part of the awakening of your multidimensional consciousness. As more DNA is turned on, you integrate your gifts and become in tune with your higher purpose.

The seven subtle bodies of the aura, starting just outside the skin, are:

» Etheric layer—energizes the physical body and provides vitality. When out of balance, physical health will decline. Associated with the root chakra.

   Strengthen: Try breathwork, yoga, and meditation.

» Emotional layer—holds emotions, feelings, and desires. Negative emotions will create disturbances in the physical body. Associated with the sacral chakra.

   Strengthen: Feel your emotions and transmute any energy from lower emotions. Focus on love, compassion, forgiveness, and opening the heart chakra.

» Mental layer—holds thought patterns, ego, judgments, and attitudes. Negative and destructive thinking will create distortions in the emotional and physical bodies, and block connection to Source and cocreation. Connected to the solar plexus chakra.

   Strengthen: Focus on being present; be conscious of your thought patterns and choose to direct them to positive thinking. Try shadow work. Release judgments and fear-based thoughts.

» Astral layer—bridge between physical and spiritual layers, the astral plane, and travels during dreamtime. Relates to relationships,

well-being, and balance. Associated with the heart chakra.

   Strengthen: Do things that bring you joy and peace, and practice gratitude and compassion.

» Spiritual layer—higher etheric template, connected to personality, creativity, and higher potential. Associated with the throat chakra.

   Strengthen: Try sound healing, chanting, singing, and praying.

» Celestial layer—emotional template of our higher emotions, wisdom, and intuition. Represents enlightenment and higher sensory perception. Associated with the third eye chakra.

   Strengthen: Try dance, neutral observation, and having unconditional love.

» Ketheric layer—universal consciousness, higher frequencies, and divine energy. Represents oneness and unity. Associated with the crown chakra.

   Strengthen: Being of service, be your authentic self and step into your soul's purpose.

Your energy bodies are constantly giving you information. When an individual comes into your presence and interacts with your energy field, you can sense how you feel around them. Even before any words are spoken, you can intuit the silent energetic exchange.

Once you learn to get in touch with the subtleties of your own "auric vision," you will better understand how energetic information is conveyed to you. Check in with yourself. Do you feel drained or uplifted when you have interacted with this person? Observe

MASCULINE AND FEMININE ENERGIES

The masculine and feminine energies exist within all of us. The left side of the body is the energetic receiving, feminine side. The right side of the body is the masculine, transmitting side.

The feminine principle is non-linear, right brained, emotional, intuitive, and creative. The male principle is linear, left brained, logical, and practical. Humanity is collectively and individually healing the masculine and feminine. Integrating and balancing both polarities within, heals the aura and unifies our Divine feminine and Divine masculine.

how you feel in their presence. Do they seem open or contracted? This information will allow you to discern whether they resonate in alignment with you or not.

This can also be applied during shamanic journeying when you encounter spirits and also to situations where you are trying to make a decision about something. Feel into the energetic signature of the situation and determine whether it is in resonance and aligned with you. Always go with your first feeling and avoid over-rationalizing your feelings with your mind. The instinctive, intuitive feeling is usually the right one. If something doesn't resonate and feel right, then you can make the choice not to engage with it; you don't always need to know why.

Soul Loss and the Aura

Your mind, emotions, and health have a profound effect on the condition of your aura. Although thoughts, feelings, and emotions possess no physical aspect you can see or touch—just like your subtle energetic body—you know they're real and also forms of energy. Stressful life circumstances, illnesses, or traumas can cause the subtle energy bodies to weaken, become misaligned, and fragmented. When a part of your soul fragments due to trauma, this is also known as soul loss. A person loses aspects of their vital energy. This is often a coping mechanism. When a traumatic event occurs, parts of the soul, or the subconscious, may retreat or separate itself so that you can survive the trauma and continue to endure everyday life.

Think of the aura as an invisible bubble all around you; this unique atmosphere energizes and protects you from unbeneficial outside influences. When you experience soul loss, there are holes and leaks in your bubble, causing this force field around you to weaken. Because of this, you have less energy, and you are more vulnerable to outside influences that can easily penetrate you. This weakens both your physical and your mental body.

Soul loss and energy leaks are losses of personal power. Some symptoms of soul loss can be depression, chronic health issues, addictions, grief that doesn't resolve, feeling outside of your body, and post-traumatic stress disorder. How do you know whether you have a weakened aura? You might feel ungrounded, anxious, exhausted, or disconnected.

It is possible through meditation, spending time in nature, journaling, forming your intentions and prayers, and doing shadow work that you can uncover what caused your soul pieces to fragment.

Energy Leaks and Loss of Power

A strong auric field is essential to your health and well-being. Even the best of us can be susceptible to outside forces and energy leaks within our own energy field. Holes, tears, energetic cords, and blockages will compromise our aura. Because we are energetic beings, the harmful electromagnetic frequencies (EMFs) we are exposed to in the environment from Wi-Fi and electronics can weaken our energy body and physical body; this can cause serious health issues. Our aura can also be weakened by negative thought forms, addictions, drugs, alcohol, destructive habits, manipulation by media, accidents, trauma, and abuse.

How can you gauge areas where you might be losing personal power? Think of instances when you could be giving power away to others that make you vulnerable to energetic leakages. What does it mean to "give your power away"? Any time you do not act or speak in congruence with your truth or who you are, you are giving your power away.

Here are common situations where we often yield or surrender our highest capabilities and noblest truths:

» Pleasing others to receive approval

» Not speaking up

» Sacrificing your wants and needs for others or focusing on martyrdom

» Allowing people to take advantage of you

» Diminishing your individual gifts and talents to fit in with others

» Doing something that you know is not in alignment with what you really want to do

Personal sovereignty is when you call your power back to yourself. When you begin to know your true self, you develop trust in making choices that are right for you. To be sovereign is to be free, because you know that you have free will. You are not acting out of pressure, societal norms, or the need to please others or fit in. When you acknowledge and activate the supreme power within yourself, you take full responsibility for your actions and you take full control over your body, mind, and spirit. Being sovereign does not cause anyone harm and allows others their right to be sovereign.

Set boundaries with the people in your life. Avoid people who drain your energy—it may be necessary to cut them out of your life for a period of time. Listen to your heart and your intuition, and make decisions based on your truth. Be honest and gentle with yourself. Cleaning and decluttering areas of your home or office can also reinstate vital energy back to your life. Simplify and remove all that no longer serves you or the person you want to become.

Take accountability for your thoughts, actions, and choices. Being sovereign reinforces your right to individuality and allows others to have their own experiences. When you refuse to give your power away, it strengthens the connection to your own inner divinity.

Protecting your aura from outside influences will keep your vital energy strong. When we are outside in the world, our energy fields are exposed and are interacting with those around us on a constant basis. We inadvertently pick up energies and, if they are not cleansed, these energies that are not harmonious will affect us. Many of us are empaths, which means we feel the emotions of others deeply, as if they were our own. We literally take them on and may not realize they are not our own. Learning how to protect

yourself from others' energy will give you a clear, balanced, and strong energy field.

While we can take steps to minimize our vulnerability to energy leaks, the reality is that we are bombarded by energetic influences every day. Learning how to cleanse, protect, and maintain a healthy aura is therefore essential to restore vitality and wholeness to your energy system.

How to Cleanse and Maintain a Strong Auric Field

One of the best ways you can cleanse and strengthen your aura is by being in nature. You can also strengthen your aura through meditation, grounding to the earth, being in sunlight, energetic cleansing in salt baths, and smudging with sage. There are crystals for cleansing the aura and for protection (see page 101). Shield yourself by visualizing a protective bubble of gold light around you. You can call your energy back to you and clear up energy leaks by connecting to your inner self through prayer, ceremony, self-love, and self-care. You can practice acceptance, forgiveness, and speaking decrees (see page 175). With a strong sense of self, you can stand in your power and speak your truth.

Traditional physical exercise such as yoga, dance, and tai chi can help move stagnant energy in the body. Sound healing and vocalizing through singing or chanting mantras can also help elevate our vibration and heal our auric field (see page 141). There is also extreme comfort and power in sitting in ceremony with other like-minded people. Together, a spiritually minded group of women and men can enhance and raise the energetic field around them. Many studies have shown the positive effects of large groups of people meditating or praying at the same time.

The Chakras

Chakras are energy vortexes. They draw in life force energy from nature, a divine energy also known as *chi* or *prana*. Each chakra has a unique quality and function, governing different areas of the physical body and endocrine glands. The chakras allow energy to flow in and out of the body, distributing the vital force that sustains life. They are invisible in nature but play a very key part in keeping you healthy and balanced.

The chakras allow you to understand energy by translating and interpreting the energy around you. It's like a diagnostic system. For example, when you walk into a room where people are arguing, you will feel the tension in your solar plexus chakra. This is because if you tune into it effectively, the chakra system allows you to translate, interpret, and transmute energy.

Most people cannot see the chakras with their eyes; however, with practice, many people can feel them. Chakras are electromagnetic energy fields. You are surrounded by electromagnetic frequencies from WI-FI and electronics, yet you cannot see them. Chakras are another frequency of electromagnetic energies. Consider the chakras as the front line for the human body, always working to maintain balance.

Chakras receive, transmit, and store energetic information. When we have a negative life event, the chakras store an imprint of the memories—negative thought forms, emotions, wounds, traumas, and stress. These become stagnant energies lodged in the chakras, preventing them from functioning properly. This impedes your mental, emotional, and physical health.

The chakras also store ancestral and past-life programing. This means we come into this life with blocks in our energy field starting from birth. Chakras become out of balance from the energetic imprint of negative life events, the energetic life force cannot flow naturally. The chakras can then become over-or under-activated. This can cause repetitive behaviors, unexplained fears, negative thoughts, harmful beliefs, or recurring life patterns that hold you back. For example, imbalanced energy in the root chakra may cause you to be fearful and untrusting; painful imprints that block the third eye chakra can cause you to doubt your own abilities.

Thus, it is necessary to clear the energy from your chakras to bring them into a balanced, activated state. You can do this through opening up your heart chakra, practicing meditation, being in nature, working with crystals, doing yoga, using sound healing or chanting, and creating specific intentions for each chakra. It's important to let go of things that don't serve you and cultivate forgiveness, compassion, gratitude, love, and joy.

When your chakras are clear and balanced, you are in tune with your environment. There is no interference or distortion to how you perceive and function. You can clearly discern what is right for you and you can live in full alignment with your life. You experience more harmony, inner peace, and unconditional love. You are vibrating at a higher frequency. Through a healthy, functioning chakra system, you can raise your vibration and the vibration of those around you.

The Nine Primary Chakras

Your energy body is an intricate network made up of hundreds of chakras, each interconnecting to various pathways. You have chakras on your hands and feet; even your organs have chakras. There are seven main chakras that run along the spine from the base of the spine (root chakra) to the top of the head (crown chakra). We will discuss these seven most common chakras and two other important chakras (earth star chakra and soul star chakra) that reside outside the physical body, in the etheric body.

As many indigenous prophecies have predicted since ancient times, humanity is going through an ascension. Over the next several years, humanity is progressing in its evolutionary process and is ascending to a higher levels of consciousness. As the energy rises on Earth, the frequency and colors of the energy bodies and chakras are changing and new chakras are coming online. Included below are the current chakra colors and higher frequency colors to assist in raising their frequency, along with visualizations, meditations, and crystals to clear and activate your chakras.

When the chakra system is cleared, balanced, and activated, the chakras merge together to form a pillar of crystalline, brilliant white light. This is the new chakra system with the higher-frequency opalescent colors of pastels, platinum, and gold. This unified chakra column occurs with the activation of the earth star chakra and the seven chakras along the spine of the physical body. The unified column is anchored to the earth from the earth star chakra, the column continues all the way up through the crown chakra to the soul star chakra and the chakras beyond.

Earth Star Chakra

The earth star chakra is six to twelve inches below your feet and resides outside your physical body, in the crust of the Earth. This is a vital chakra because it grounds and anchors your entire chakra system to the Earth's magnetic core and crystalline grid. Divine light and energy flow from the earth star chakra through the root chakra and into the chakra system. With this connection to the Earth, you are able to draw in the divine energy from the cosmos and integrate it in a grounded way.

The earth star chakra holds the information of all that is, including the memories of your past lives and your gifts. It is also connected to the collective consciousness of humanity. To ascend into the higher realms, it is necessary to have a solid connection to the Earth and its energy.

When the earth star chakra is out of balance, you may feel anxiousness and low on energy. You may also feel as if you are not present in the moment, and it will be very difficult to stay focused on commitments. With a clear and balanced earth star chakra, you are focused, present, and at peace. You are expressing your soul's gifts. You are in tune with your highest nature and life's purpose. Once the earth star chakra is activated, you are able to cleanse

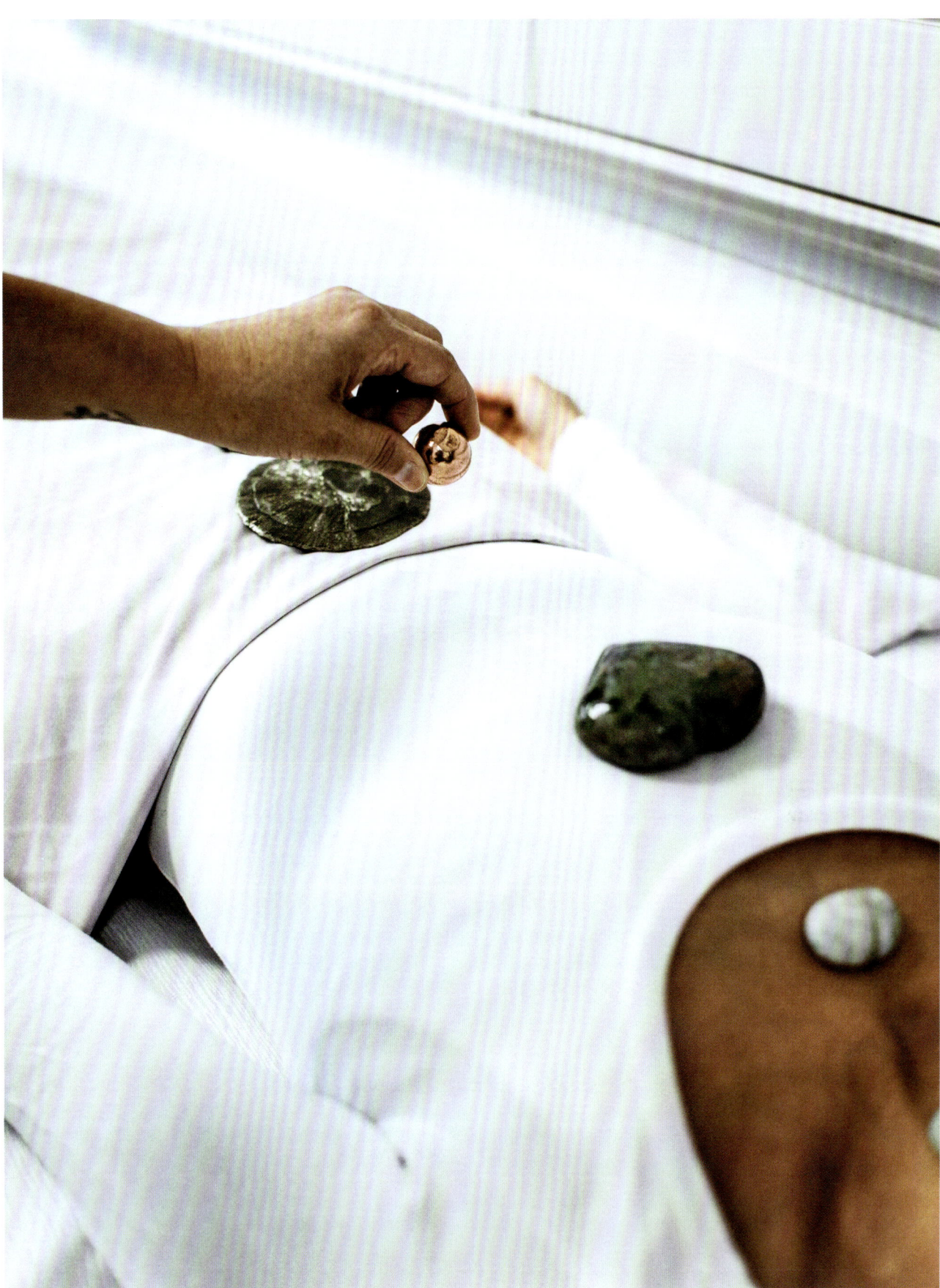

any lower vibrational energies in your chakra system and remain grounded regardless of what is going on externally. You are able to embody the "as above, so below" and all that is—within your human form.

- » COLOR: Platinum silver
- » CRYSTALS: Black kyanite, pyrite, angel aura quartz
- » MANTRA: I am anchored to Mother Earth.
- » VISUALIZATION: Begin by tuning into and feeling your connection with the Earth. Send love, gratitude, and reverence to the Earth for all the support. Imagine sending platinum silver roots from the base of your spine (root chakra) about six inches into the crust of the Earth. Wrap the roots around your earth star chakra. Visualize the silver energy of your earth star chakra and see it as a silver sphere. Now imagine light coming from the Earth's core flowing into your earth star charka, cleansing, clearing, and activating it. Continue bringing the divine energy up through your feet and chakra column and visualize the energy clearing anything heavy or stagnant. Do this all the way to your crown chakra. See your entire chakra column aligned as one pillar of white diamond light.

Root Chakra

The root chakra is at the base of the spine and in the pelvic area. It is connected to the unconscious mind and associated with survival, security, and safety. It keeps you grounded to the Earth and helps you be present, centered, and energized. When the root chakra is out of balance, you may feel fearful, unsafe, and disconnected. With a clear and balanced root chakra, you love yourself; feel secure, stable, and grateful; and trust in life.

- » COLOR: Wine red
- » CRYSTALS: Black tourmaline, apatite, jade
- » MANTRA: I am safe to step into my brilliance and mastery.
- » VISUALIZATION: Close your eyes and imagine your root chakra filling with a shimmering blue-green-aqua color. If you see any red color or dense energy, continue to clear and transmute it with the higher vibrational color of iridescent blue-green-aqua.

Sacral Chakra

The sacral chakra is located just below the navel and is associated with creativity, sexuality, relationships, abundance, and productivity. Your intuition, gut feeling, and womb wisdom resides in the sacral chakra. Connected to the emotional body, this chakra can carry sexual traumas and imprints from our ancestors or any sexual abuse. When out of balance, shame, unworthiness, and self-doubt will reside here. There will be issues with sexuality, creative endeavors, and following through with projects. A clear and balanced sacral chakra shows healthy sexual expression, creative flow, joy, and positive relationships.

- » COLOR: Orange
- » CRYSTALS: Orange or pink calcite, sunstone, rose quartz
- » MANTRA: I am free to express my true self.
- » VISUALIZE: Imagine a pinkish rose-colored energy in your heart chakra and draw it down

into your entire pelvic area. Infuse this area with love and allow the pink energy to fill it, clearing any heavy energy and transmuting any orange color.

Solar Plexus Chakra

The solar plexus chakra is in between the rib cage. It is associated with the ego, personal power, willpower, and vitality. Our confidence and authenticity reside here. This chakra allows you to assess and feel the energies of your environment and other people. When this chakra is not functioning properly, you may experience anger, be judgmental, lack boundaries, have low energy, and lack willpower. When the solar plexus chakra is clear and balanced, it is easy to express your emotions and needs and you have a strong sense of self and sense of purpose.

» **COLOR:** Yellow
» **CRYSTALS:** Citrine, pyrite, healers gold
» **MANTRA:** I am a master of my own energy.
» **VISUALIZATION:** Close your eyes and take some deep breaths, bringing all your awareness into your body. Now scan your entire energy field and sense if you are leaking any energy or power. Sense beyond your energy body to see if your energy is scattered anywhere else. Tune into your solar plexus area. Consciously call all your energy back to your body. Feel and visualize this energy coming back into your solar plexus and energy body. Continue this process while imagining your solar plexus filling with sparking gold light. Do this anytime you feel a loss of power.

Heart Chakra

The heart chakra is your access to pure love: your ability to receive love and give love, without conditions. Your heart chakra allows you to be empathetic and compassionate and is the bridge between the lower chakras and the upper chakras, where the physical meets the spiritual. A heart chakra that is unbalanced cannot feel love. It can carry sadness and emotional issues. With a balanced heart chakra, you feel united with others and connected to life. You have compassion and can forgive others and be at peace. When your heart chakra is activated, your intuition will come from the heart center.

Also known as the divine gate, the heart chakra is the core of the ascension process, which occurs through an activated and open heart chakra and connects you to the upper chakras. This gives you access to your gifts, connection to your Higher Self, and a knowing that a universal divine and omnipresent force exists everywhere and that you have access to this higher power.

» **COLOR:** Green/pink
» **CRYSTALS:** Celestite, larimar, chrysocolla
» **MANTRA:** I am pure divine love.
» **VISUALIZATION:** Imagine sparkly diamond white light pouring from your soul star chakra down into your heart chakra. Allow the diamond white light to cleanse away any heavy or stuck energies. Bring in an aqua-green-blue color and feel gratitude in your heart.

THE POWER OF YOUR HEART

The heart is the most powerful source of electromagnetic energy in the human body. The heart's electrical field is sixty times greater in amplitude then the electrical field generated by the brain. Through your emotional state, you can affect your energy field and the environment around you. By shifting your emotions, to feelings of gratitude and appreciation, you can shift your energetic state and dissolve stress, frustration, anxiety, irritation, and the fight-or-flight response. When the heart chakra is activated, you have an open heart filled with love and compassion. From this very powerful activated heart space you align with your inner self. Your choices and actions come from your truth, sovereignty, and being of service.

Throat Chakra

The throat chakra represents communication, speaking your truth, and self-expression. You manifest your words into reality through what you say. Self-sovereignty is connected to the throat chakra, because you speak the truth of your soul. When you authentically speak from your soul, your words carry vibrational codes of information that can positively affect yourself and those around you. If the throat chakra is unbalanced, you will have difficulty expressing yourself and the energy of your speech can negatively affect yourself and others. You will have difficulty manifesting your desires. With a balanced throat chakra, you can listen and express yourself well and speak with authenticity, integrity, and confidence.

- » **COLOR:** Blue
- » **CRYSTALS:** Kyanite, mica, and lapis lazuli
- » **MANTRA:** I speak the truth of my soul.
- » **VISUALIZATION:** Imagine a diamond white light coming down from your soul star chakra, cleansing your throat and releasing any imprints or blockages. Affirm that you release any energies, agreements, or contracts from any lifetime that are preventing you from expressing your soul. Now activate your throat chakra—bring in a silver platinum color.

Third Eye Chakra

Third eye chakra is on the forehead between the eyes. The third eye gives you access to other dimensions and your psychic abilities. It is where you receive your intuition, imagination, and wisdom. Through this chakra, you visualize what you want to manifest in your life. An unbalanced third eye will lead to confusion and fear of success. It will be difficult for you to have clarity and see the bigger picture. When balanced, you will be connected to your intuition and will find your visions are manifesting in the physical world.

- » COLOR: Indigo
- » CRYSTALS: Azurite, shattuckite, labradorite
- » MANTRA: I see with clarity.
- » VISUALIZATION: Spend a few minutes when you wake up and before you go to bed with your eyes closed, focusing your physical eyes up to look at your third eye. Visualize a rainbow of colors in your third eye. Now bring the vision of something you want to manifest into your third eye. If you are not already a visual person, you might not see anything visually to start, but the energy of that intention is still there. Over time, you might find you see colors and eventually see visions.

Crown Chakra

The crown chakra is at the top of the head and gives you access to the collective unconscious, the wisdom of your soul, your Higher Self, and oneness. The function of the petals of the crown chakra is to bring higher frequencies into your third eye. When the crown chakra is unbalanced, you may feel disconnected to your spirit and the higher realms or you may feel totally ungrounded in your body. You can be too much in your head. When your crown chakra is balanced, you will feel connected to your inner wisdom and purpose and to others and life, and you will feel a sense of joy, serenity, and wholeness.

- » COLOR: Purple or white
- » CRYSTALS: Clear quartz, lemurian quartz, andara crystals
- » MANTRA: I am connected to Source.
- » VISUALIZE: Imagine liquid gold light pouring down from above you and into your crown chakra. Allow the liquid gold to purify your connection to the Divine above you.

Soul Star Chakra

The soul star chakra is located six inches above your crown chakra, residing within your aura. This chakra stores the information of all your lifetimes and contains the blueprint to all of your spiritual gifts. Your soul star chakra is connected to your Higher Self and the light of the cosmos. If your soul star chakra is unbalanced, you may feel confusion, depression, and paranoia. When it is balanced and activated, your lower chakras will be balanced and activated as well. This chakra will give you access to psychic abilities, divine love, and direct knowing from your Higher Self.

- » COLOR: Magenta
- » CRYSTALS: Selenite, celestite, auralite 23
- » MANTRA: I transcend.
- » VISUALIZE: Imagine sending energy up from your earth star chakra to your heart chakra, through your crown chakra, and connecting up to your soul star chakra. Sense the higher vibrational energy above you and bring it back down, anchoring it into your heart chakra. Ask questions that you want clarity about.

Heart-Brain Quick Coherence Technique

This simple process will bring you into a state of coherence where creativity, joy, clarity, and inner guidance are accessed with ease.

Quick Coherence® Technique

1. Focus your attention in the area of the heart. Imagine your breath is flowing in and out of your heart or chest area, breathing a little slower and deeper than usual. Find an easy rhythm that's comfortable.

2. As you continue heart-focused breathing, make a sincere attempt to experience a regenerative feeling such as appreciation or care for someone or something in your life.

Quick Steps

1. Heart-Focused Breathing
2. Activate a positive or renewing feeling

You can practice several times a day whenever you notice any tension or resistance. Do the steps for at least 3 minutes or longer to get the most benefit. The Quick Coherence Technique was created by the HeartMath Institute, whose extensive scientific studies show that heart–brain coherence has numerous health benefits, including lowering cortisol, reducing stress, and decreasing anxiety. You can also touch the center of your chest at the heart chakra, this brings your awareness from your thinking mind into your heart center. A coherent state brings the mind, body, and emotions into alignment. In this coherent and harmonized state you are able to access your inner being and intuition.

Meditation to Activate All the Chakras & Aura

Find a quiet space in nature and sit on the earth. This is the best way to connect to your earth star chakra. If this is not possible, find a quiet space in your home.

Create a sacred space and call in any spirit helpers (see page 67).

Set the intention to bring your energy fields into their highest vibrational state. Send a beam of light up through your crown chakra, past your soul star chakra and connect to source energy above you. Bring the energy back down through the top of your head (crown chakra), and bathe each chakra in this higher vibrational energy. This activates each chakra. If you feel any heavy energy in your body or chakras use this light energy to cleanse it.

Continue sending the energy down into the earth and anchor into the earth star chakra, continue to send the energy deep into the earth's crystalline core. Visualize your entire chakra system as one column of diamond white light.

Now imagine drawing energy up through your root chakra and into your heart center. Take a deep breath through your heart. Imagine you are breathing through the center of your heart chakra, sending your breath and energy into the layers of your auric field. Continue to infuse light energy and breath from your heart chakra into your aura.

Feel and visualize your aura expanding and energizing. Notice the strength and protection created with your breath and energy. You now have cleared and activated your chakras and aura. This can be a beneficial daily practice. Close the sacred space and give thanks to any spirit guides and helpers.

ENERGETIC CORD CUTTING

We can have energetic cords attached to people, places, and things. When we have intimate relationships, emotional experiences, and traumatic experiences energetic attachments can continue to keep us connected by a cord. These cords create a drain on our vital energy. And, because all of our lifetimes are occurring simultaneously, cords can also be attached to events in other realities. When this occurs, fragments of our energy remain attached in that timeline.

Cord Cutting Technique

Find a comfortable and quiet place. Open up sacred space and call in your Higher Self. State your intention to cut any energetic cords that are draining your energy. Bring your awareness fully into your body in a relaxed state. Ask whether you have any cords attached to anyone that might be leaking your energy. See if anyone's name, face, or energy comes into your awareness. Or, think about any person or situation that you have an emotional charge around and bring that into your awareness. Now visualize or feel them in front of you. Scan your energy body and chakras—often you can feel where in the body or which chakra the cord is attached. Sense or visualize the cords between you. Using the side or your hand, or a crystal or shamanic knife as a tool—sever the cord attached to you and send the energy back to the person with love. You can also visualize the cord being cut with a knife or scissors. Scan again as there may be more than one cord. Once you have released the cord, seal the area where you cut the cord with gold light. Repeat the process with the cords that are still attached to the other person, place or thing. Imagine your energy body enveloped in gold or silver light. Give gratitude and close the space.

Part II
TOOLS FROM THE NATURAL AND UNSEEN WORLDS

05
Creating Sacred Space and Introducing Ceremony

Living a shamanic lifestyle involves bringing shamanic practices and ceremonies into our everyday life. Engaging in ritual and ceremony is an outward expression of our internal state; it is a way to anchor our intentions and send them out into the invisible realms. When we step away from the hustle and bustle of everyday life, we are making a purposeful effort to connect with our spiritual selves. These practices are intentional and sacred, as they bridge the ordinary with the divine.

A shamanic ceremony typically includes one or more of the four elements (such as a sacred water or fire ceremony) or the use of drumming and musical instruments. Shamans tell stories, sing songs, pray, chant, dance, and use many talents at their disposal to express their gratitude and respect for Mother Earth, along with their spirit allies.

Ceremony anchors you in the present moment and creates a higher degree of self-awareness, which will reveal the thoughts, feelings, actions, and patterns that you're operating from. Ceremony allows you to go within and reconnect with your body, soul, and Higher Self, while also strengthening your connection to nature, the elements, and the spirit world. The more you align with the Universal Source, the more you align with your highest purpose—what the shamans call your sacred dream. Shamans believe we are all dreaming our world into being, meaning we are creating our own reality. Ceremony allows you to release the energies, programing, and beliefs that are preventing you from living your fullest potential. When you are in alignment with your Higher Self, you step into your sacred dream and powerfully create your own reality.

Setting up sacred space and offering prayers are the foundation of ceremonies and are woven into every aspect of shamanism. By creating and entering a place that focuses our mental, physical, and spiritual alignment, we can reach wellness at all levels.

Setting Sacred Space

Shamans begin every ceremony and healing practice by setting sacred space. The veil that obstructs your view of the spirit world is thinner in sacred space, giving potency to your intentions and prayers. When you open up sacred space, you are directing your energy into the present moment and calling in your spirit helpers to assist in protecting your container for your intentions and prayers. Whether you speak them aloud or hold them within your heart, you call in and command the unseen energies into your sacred space.

Sacred space may be created anywhere—indoors or in nature—and it may be any size—big or small. Sacred space may even be a space within—a state of being that you carry with you everywhere.

It's less important where and what size your sacred space is and more important that you're being mindful when setting it. Creating sacred space is a very personal practice. How one individual creates theirs may differ completely from another person's process, neither of which is right or wrong. Operating from the heart with authenticity and for your highest good are key principles.

Setting up sacred space can involve a simple process of saying a prayer and setting intentions just before your ceremonial or healing work; when the work is complete, the sacred space is then closed. Creating a sacred space can also involve setting up a sacred altar that serves as a physical place to say prayers, anchor and amplify intentions, create beauty, bring protection, and raise the vibration of the space. Altars can be left in a place in the home or can be used for a specific ceremony and taken down when the ceremony is finished.

Whether you have a simple sacred space or a sacred altar, calling in the Four Directions, Mother Earth, Father Sky, Creator, and any additional spirits, allies, guardians, guides, or ancestors that you'd like to work with, will bring energy and power into your ceremony, ritual, or healing practice. After it is complete, you will close the sacred space in a similar manner, by thanking and honoring the energies you called in.

Setting Up a Simple Sacred Space

This process creates a sacred space before your ceremonies, rituals, and healing practices, including meditation and prayer.

1. Find a quiet space you can use, without being disturbed.

2. Clear any clutter from the space that could obstruct your intentions and prayers. Use a cloth, blanket, or cushion to make your experience as comfortable as possible.

3. Burn one or two candles in the space, to focus the energy.

4. Cleanse (smudge) yourself and the space with sage or palo santo.

5. Clear your mind so you can be fully present—use singing bowls, drumming, chimes, bells, rattles, or song to drop into your heart and immerse yourself in the unseen world.

6. Say your prayers, state your intentions, and call in any helping spirits (see page 72).

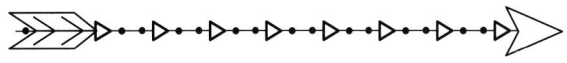

Building a Sacred Altar

Setting up a sacred altar is an ancient practice of creating sacred space in your home or wherever you are. An altar is a gateway to the divine that brings beauty and spiritual energy, it can be used for ceremony, ritual, and healing. There is no right or wrong way to set up your sacred altar, as long as you are operating from the heart and with your highest good in mind.

The items required to set up your sacred altar include:

» An altar cloth: preferably cotton or silk

» Crystals: black tourmaline, lapis lazuli, clear quartz, amethyst, etc.

» Sacred items: photos, animal figures, deities, etc.

» Offerings: fruits, sweets, or flowers

» Sacred herbs: white sage, palo santo, or sweetgrass

» Candles: beeswax or another natural burning wax

» Essential oils: protection spray, vetiver, etc.

» Feathers and an abalone shell

» Matches or a lighter

Here are a few simple steps for setting up your sacred altar:

1. Find a private space in your home, on a raised surface. Cover the surface with an altar cloth or other piece of material that means something to you.

2. Gather crystals and other sacred objects you wish to place on the altar; use any items that are magickal, powerful, or sentimental to you. Let your intuition guide you in placing the crystals and sacred objects on your altar. Place each item with a specific intention in mind. Think of your crystals as living entities that take instruction. When you give them an intention to serve, they do so by amplifying that intention out into the universe.

3. Place an offering on your altar, to honor your ancestors.

4. Place any additional items such as candles, essential oils, feathers, or shells on your altar.

5. Smudge yourself and the space with your sacred herbs to clear any stagnant or unwanted energies.

You now have a sacred space that works quietly to magnify your intentions and aligns with the power of the universe, while also serving as a reminder of the energies you're calling in. Use your altar for: ceremony, meditation, prayer, offering gratitude and however else you are guided to work with it.

NOTE: There may also be times when you want to build a new altar to denote a new phase or transition in your life, the change of seasons (solstice equinox), a new year, a birthday, a new career, an engagement, or a new business launch. Whatever the reason, always set up your new altar with intentions that are unique to you.

The Four Directions, Mother Earth, and Father Sky

Calling in the Four Directions, Mother Earth, and Father Sky involves calling in various aspects of Spirit. It is a pivotal part in setting up sacred space for ceremony, ritual, and healing, and multiple cultures agree that honoring the directions is an integral part of performing any sacred work.

The Four Directions are the spirit guardians of your space, enabling you to anchor your body and soul in the center of the universe. Father Sky, Mother Earth, and the Creator are also called in, to connect you above, below, and center. Together they form the Seven Directions of Sacred Space.

All around the globe, and since ancient times, the Four Directions—south, west, east, and north—have been honored and recognized as sacred archetypal energies. The ancients named the directions based on their surroundings, language, and culture, and as such, there are many ways of working with the directions, depending on the tradition being followed. Different cultures and tribes have different archetypes, elements, colors, and animals associated with each direction. The importance lies in recognizing and working with these energies, not in how we identify them. Intention is everything.

Invocation of the Directions

Developing your own words and approach for calling in and honoring the directions is more potent than following phrases that don't come from your heart. You can call in the directions out loud or in silence.

You can stand and face each direction with your hands open. You can shake a rattle toward each direction, or you can sit comfortably with your eyes closed in meditation. Again, intention is the key.

The more you work with the directions, the more you'll be guided to do so in a way that is unique to you. Until that time arrives, here is an example of how you can invoke the Four Directions, Mother Earth, and Father Sky.

South

To the spirits of the south, the fire element, the Great Serpent, I call you into this space. Show me how to transmute and transform the past like the way you shed your skin. I call in the fire element: teach me to shine so brightly that my passion is inspiration to others. I call in Sekhmet, the lioness: bring healing and light into this space. Thank you, and so it is, Aho.

South Altar Suggestions

» Candle, fire (in cauldron), incense, the color red, image of the Sun

» Crystal pyramid or obsidian object

» Figurine of a jaguar, lion, Sekhmet, Pele, snake, sun, dragon, phoenix

» Essential oils: frankincense, dragon's blood, cinnamon

» Crystals: ruby, carnelian, fire opal

West

Hail to the west, Mother Jaguar, I invite you into this space. Help me to see my shadows and fears so I can let go of my stories. I call to the Orcas; I ask you to teach me how to walk without fear of death and to embrace the cycles of life. Water element: show me how to flow with the cycles of life; I honor you. Thank you, and so it is, Aho.

West Altar Suggestions

» Blue items, heart-shaped crystals, yoni egg, crystal ball, Ankh, shell

» Goblet/cup/chalice/bowl of water, pictures of body of water. The color blue or green.

» Figurine of mermaid or divine feminine

» Essential oils: rose, vetiver, ylang-ylang

» Crystals: larimar, aquamarine, black kyanite

North

I call to the spirits of the north, the earth element, I invite you here, protect this healing space. Great Owl, show me your wisdom and knowledge; be here. I call in my ancestors, teach me the courage to endure life's challenges. Ancient ones, be here with me, I honor you. Thank you, and so it is, Aho.

North Altar Suggestions

» Food, stones, soil, trees, plants, acorn, money

» Images of trees, mountains

» Bone or horn

» Figurine of hummingbirds, owl, Gaia, wolf, buffalo, Isis, color green, black, or red

» Essential oils: patchouli, cypris, cedarwood

» Crystals: black tourmaline, shungite, chrysocolla

East

Spirits of the east, great Eagle/Condor, I invite you into this space, bring me up into your wings so I may fly with the Great Spirit, wing tip to wing tip—reaching my highest destiny. Air element, teach me your wisdom, let me understand the great mysteries, I welcome you. Thank you, and so it is, Aho.

East Altar Suggestions

» White sage, sandalwood, incense, feathers, flowers/plants, songs, written prayers, or words

» Ritual knife, sword, wind chimes/Koshi chimes

» Figure of eagle, owl, or Kuan Yin, picture of the sun, birds, or clouds, the color yellow

» Essential oils: peppermint, citrus, lemongrass

» Crystals: citrine, fluorite, celestite

Mother Earth

I call to our Mother Earth, thank you for providing support for all life on Earth. I invite the energies of the stones, the crystals, the little people, and the elemental kingdom.

Father Sky

I call to Father Sky, the Sun, Moon, and stars. Spirit helpers, guides, guardians, angels, and ancestors, I invite you into this space. Bring us healing, guidance, and protection. Thank you, and so it is, Aho.

Creator

Creator, Great Spirit, God, Christ, I invite you into this space, thank you for the wisdom of my heart and soul. Thank you for this sacred life. Thank you, and so it is, Aho.

Working with the Four Directions, Mother Earth, Father Sky, and Creator brings balance and spiritual growth into your life. Alongside calling in these energies when setting sacred space, you are also encouraged to call in any other divine support in the form of spirits, allies, guides, guardians, and ancestors that you'd like to work with.

NOTE: These invocations call in the Seven Directions of Sacred Space through an amalgamation of many traditions. The altar suggestions give you a range of options and symbols for each. As you develop your own relationship with the energies, you will realize your own meaning for them and may even place them in a different direction. There is no wrong way to do this.

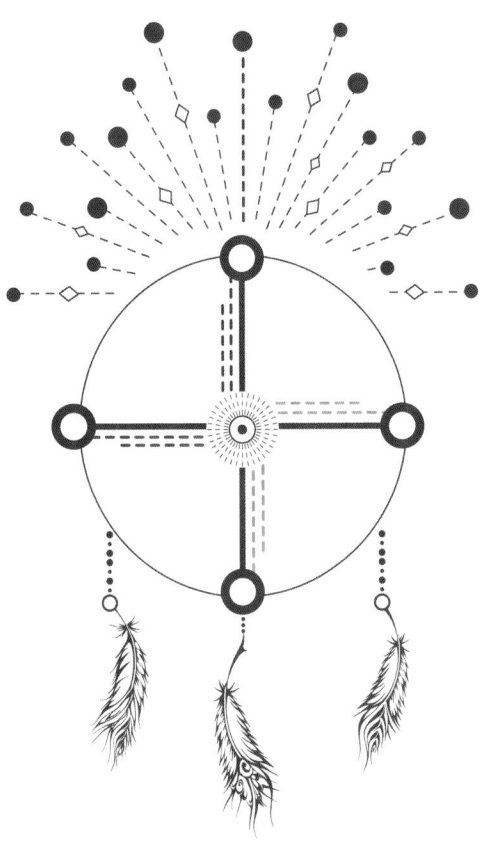

Helping Spirits, Guides, Allies, and Ancestors

What you see with your eyes in this three-dimensional world we are all experiencing, is not all there is. You are living in a multidimensional world, surrounded by helping spirits, allies, guides, guardians, and ancestors who can support and protect you. They can only communicate with you if and when you ask them to—you must have the intention to communicate with them.

Keep in mind that guides, guardians, and spirit allies can be viewed as an extension of your Higher Self—that may appear to you in the form of a spirit helper so you are able to perceive them. You might wish to practice connecting directly with your Higher Self and inner Source. Still, connecting with ancestors and spirit helpers can be a beneficial practice. Learning to communicate with them takes practice. Asking them to work with you and help you in realizing your intentions takes gratitude and a sincere intention to work with humility and universal love.

Energy is everything, including communication. Delivered and received information is a form of communication, and therefore a form of energy. We all perceive the energy of and communication from the spirit world differently; we all have a unique way of connecting to spirits and receiving their message. Some of us receive our messages visually, some of us hear them, some of us feel them, some of us smell them, some of us taste them; some of us may not see, hear, feel, smell, or taste them, but have a strong sense of knowing the message being delivered. Still others receive spirit world messages in a combination of these ways or through higher sensory perceptions for example, telepathy. It doesn't matter how you receive a message; what matters most is that you're open to receiving it.

These different forms of receiving information from the spirit world are considered *clair senses*, and they correspond to the six senses: seeing, hearing, feeling, smelling, tasting, and knowing. Most of us have one clair sense that is more dominant than the others. To communicate with the spirit world, it is helpful to determine what your dominant clair sense is:

Clairvoyance means clear seeing.

Clairaudience means clear hearing

Clairsentience means clear feeling.

Clairalience means clear smelling.

Clairgustance means clear tasting.

Claircognizance means clear knowing.

Meditation for Discovering Your Dominant Clair

Here's a great practice for discovering your dominant clair.

Set up a sacred space. Call in your spiritual team and your Higher Self, ask for protection while clearing the energies of the space using sounds or herbs.

Sit or lie down in a comfortable position with your eyes closed. Take three deep breaths in through your nose and out through your mouth.

Imagine a beam of light traveling from the root chakra (at the base of your spine) into the Earth and feel yourself connect and get grounded with Mother Earth. Stay grounded, while directing that same light energy back up through the root, sacral, and solar plexus chakras, clearing each one as it makes its way to the heart chakra.

Focus a moment on the heart chakra, taking a deep breath in and out through your nose. Imagine that the breath is coming through the center of your heart. Send the energy up through the top of your head, open up the crown chakra, allowing yourself to connect to the higher vibrational energy field above your head. Continue to send your energy upwards until you feel your eyes flutter.

Set your intention to connect to one of your spirits, allies, guides, guardians, ancestors, or your Higher Self. Invite spirits who come in unconditional love and for your highest good.

Clear your mind of lingering thoughts or feelings from the day, so you may receive the information more clearly. State out loud or silently, "I call my spirit guide into this space. I would like to establish a relationship and have a dialogue of clear communication with you."

Be present and observe what comes to you. Pay attention to any colors, sounds, smells, tastes, or feelings. If you feel a sensation, the presence of something, warmth, or tingling, that is a sign of clairsentience. If you hear something, you could be dominant in clairaudience. If you see images or pictures in your mind's eye, that's a sign of clairvoyance, and so on. Pay attention to what comes up first—that will be your dominant clair.

Don't judge or rationalize what you receive; the meaning will come to you over time if it isn't clear in the moment. Always give gratitude and appreciation for what you receive.

Write about what comes up for you. A regular writing practice will help you solidify your experiences. Do this exercise daily until you've established your dominant clair. Be patient, as establishing an initial relationship can take time. Trust and have faith in what you receive.

Once you know your dominant clair, you can continue to meditate to establish a deeper relationship with your helping spirits and also to connect with your weaker clairs. As you develop clear communication with your spirit helpers, your relationships will deepen.

What to Be Aware of When You Are Communicating with the Spirit World

FREE WILL: Not all spirits and ancestors you come into contact with will be there for your highest good. There are lower vibrational spirits that will have their own agendas. A true helping spirit will never try to make you go against your free will. If the spirit is pressuring you to go against your free will, then it's most likely a lower vibrational spirit and not a true guide. Always ask for protection before engaging with the spirit world.

INTUITION: Trust your instincts when working with spirits. Let them earn your trust as you develop a relationship with them. Always ask for your highest good but start by asking simple questions that aren't life altering. Sit with the information provided, apply it, and gauge the results. If the interaction doesn't feel good, you can disengage and tell them to leave.

There are many ways your helping spirits, allies, guides, guardians, and ancestors will communicate with you, and it might not come during the meditation itself. Keep requesting assistance and asking questions, and leave the lines of communication open. Pay attention to the signs and symbols around you: some of the ways you'll receive your message will be in numerical sequences, through life's synchronicities, in your dreams, in music, in books, via animals, and through your intuitive pings.

The Power of Prayer

The spirit world is where the many helping spirits reside: nature spirits, the spirits of the animal, mineral, and plant kingdoms, guides and guardians, angels, holy figures, dragons, deities, star beings, and more. The Great Spirit, Creator, God, Christ, Universal Source, and Divine are interchangeable and represent the source energy field of all that is. This zero point energy field of divine love, exists within and all around you, and with it you can cocreate your reality through prayer.

Prayer is an empowering shamanic practice that brings your intentions—the things you want—into reality. Working with the spirit world and the Great Spirit for the highest good is central to leading a shamanic way of life. Prayer opens the doorway to the unseen world and is a direct vehicle for communication between your Higher Self and the Great Spirit.

From the simple to the miraculous, you must ask to receive. A prayer is asking for what you desire, and when it's coming from your heart with sincerity and it is for your highest good, it has the most potency. You have the free will to choose your path and to create your sacred dream—if you don't give the Great Spirit direction on what you seek, you leave your life open to chance. Through prayer, so much more can be accomplished than by trying to control outcomes. When you align with the Divine, you are aligning with the forces of creation, and prayer can shift your conscious reality at the molecular level.

Prayer can also be made for other people in our lives who might be sick or who need help, for groups, for our Earth, and for specific lands. When groups come together for a specific prayer with a clear intention, be it a healing for an individual or for the planet, the energy is magnified. When the group is praying, from the heart and for the highest good, and with emotions that reflect the healing having already taken place, the results are profound and miraculous. The extent that prayer can be used is limitless and the magnitude of results can be profound.

How to Pray

Prayer is an sacred power that is accessible to you anytime and from any space. It can be words spoken aloud or thoughts in your head, or you can pray by sending out a feeling, vibration, or visualization. Regardless of how you communicate your prayer, there is one very key universal law to follow—anything that you intend through prayer, it is important to act as if you have already received it. You do this by embodying the energy of that which you wish to bring into your life.

While you pray, deeply feel the gratitude, joy, and emotions you would feel if you already had what you are asking for. This is what activates your prayer. Then, you surrender your prayer to the Great Spirit—a higher power that knows much better than you do how to orchestrate your desires and manifest your intentions. You relinquish control and you trust in divine timing and perfection regarding the events in your life.

Once you've finished praying and as you go on with your day, you continue to think, feel, speak, and act as though your prayer has been fulfilled. In this way, your very state of being becomes your prayer. Intention and gratitude allow you to receive what you are inviting through prayer.

Prayer for Assistance and Protection

Great Spirit, I am free and clear from the limiting beliefs and patterns from this lifetime and across all lifetimes that hold me back from speaking my truth. Thank you, and so it is, Aho.

If you don't already know what you want, you can ask for what is in your highest good and the highest good of all:

Great Spirit, I call on your protection and assistance in _____ situation. I trust in your guidance and ask for the best possible outcome for the highest good of all involved.

Prayer for Clearing Space

I request my Higher Self, guardians, helping spirits, and the highest levels of light to clear, cleanse, and purify this space. To assist me in releasing all heavy, unwanted energies that are not beneficial to me in this space. I give my deepest thank you, and so it is.

Prayer for Blessing the Space

I call to the Divine Spirit within all things. I call to my team of spiritual helpers and the cosmos. I thank you for your protection and assistance. I fill this space with love, joy, and prosperity. When I walk into this sanctuary, I feel at ease and at home. The energy of this space is in harmony with my highest purpose. This space enriches my life in all areas. With heartfelt love and gratitude, I thank you. So be it, and so it is, Aho.

06
The Five Great Elements

Our ancestors knew that the universe, nature, our bodies, and the world around us is made of the four elements of creation: air, fire, water, and earth. Air represents gas, wind, movement, and change. Fire transforms states of matter into different forms—solids to liquids, liquids to gases, and back again. Water represents all liquid states of matter, and earth represents all solid states of matter. Akasha—the fifth element—enables everything to come into being and is where all matter is formed.

The five great elements are five states of matter that correspond with different energies. They are reflected in nature through the cycles you experience in the world: from the passage of the seasons, spring (air), summer (fire), fall (water), and winter (earth), to the cycles of life, destruction, death, and rebirth.

Your physical body is alive because the elements are within you. Knowledge of the elements will give you an understanding of the laws of nature, your body, and the universe. Understanding how to balance the elements within your body and your environment brings you back into a state of harmony and increases your personal power, your health, your spiritual growth, and happiness.

Air, Fire, Water, Earth, and Akasha

The ancients—the shamans, healers, magicians, and alchemists—knew that the power of the elements weaves the very fabric of creation. Around 450 BCE, the Greek philosopher, healer, and scientist Empedocles described the four elements of air, fire, water, and earth as the substances from which all physical matter arises. This became the cornerstone of the medical system, philosophies, and spiritual practices in ancient Greece. The fifth element was added by the Greek philosopher and scientist Aristotle, and it was named Aether, also known as Akasha in India, Quintessence in Europe, and in other traditions, Space, Spirit, Universal Life Force, and God.

Greece was not the only civilization that understood that all matter arises from the five elements. The elements were recognized in the ancient cultures of Persia, Egypt, Babylonia, India, China, Korea, Japan, and Tibet. The sacredness of these natural phenomena was woven into religions, such as Buddhism and Hinduism. In Buddhism, the four elements are a basis for observing ourselves to understand human suffering and how to liberate ourselves from suffering. In Hinduism, the five elements form the system of Ayurveda, a philosophy of medicine used today as an alternative health practice.

Harnessing the Power of the Elements

Attuning to the energy of the five elements enabled our ancestors to keep their bodies in balance and be in harmony with Mother Earth and the natural cycles of life, death, and rebirth. The elements give you a framework for seeing yourself and the world: they are reflected in the outside world of nature, and they are also inside ourselves, our bodies, and our spirit.

Our physical body is comprised of the chemical substances of the four elements; we are the elements. As such, the elements enable our bodies to function. Air is the breath you take. Fire gives you energy, allowing for digestion and hunger. Water is your

bodily fluids, blood, and lymph. All the solid structures in your body—teeth, bones, skin, and hair—represent the earth element. Akasha is the space your body resides in. When one element is out of balance in any way—physically or energetically— the body shifts into disharmony, leading to illness and disease. The elements are an integral part of our environment, representing everything that is within and around us. Because we are interconnected with our environment, if the elements are off, it is reflected in how our chakras function. The elements are associated with the chakras; therefore, if an element is out of balance, the corresponding chakra will be out of balance, as well as the associated area of the body.

Once you acknowledge these sacred elements, how can you work with them in your own life? From a shamanic perspective, the five elements teach us to strive for balance within ourselves and our life. Learning how to work with the elements will restore equilibrium in your body, and you will learn to better harmonize your life in all aspects. You will learn that all things exist in a continuous cycle, connected to the whole.

At the core of any ceremony or ritual is change and transformation. When you participate in ceremony, you will notice subtle and profound shifts in your life. Ceremony accesses your psyche and shifts your perspectives. The main purpose is to restore your wholeness and lift the veil between the physical and the unseen worlds. When you perform these activities from pure intention, you can connect deeply with the Universal Source.

The five great elements were revered as sacred by our earliest civilizations and were called upon for rites of purification, healing, blessing, and self-mastery. You can learn to work with the elements in the same way, through ceremony and ritual. The elements can be used to clear heavy energies from spaces or to call in higher vibrational energies of harmony and abundance. As you develop a relationship with the elements and learn to harness their power, the creative force of alchemy becomes your ally.

Air Element

Air is the vital breath of life, your life force. It is the breath of your spirit. Air represents the winds of change, flexibility, and new beginnings. It is a masculine element of communication, wisdom, and intellect. This is where we form our ideas and plans, our visions and dreams.

The air element allows us to listen to the wind for signs and divination. The spirits of the wind bring messages from the Divine. Air is connected to the sky, clouds, cosmos, the winged ones, sylphs, fairies, spirits, deities, gods, and upper realms. Air governs teaching, information, travel, computers, psychic powers, and learning. This element represents the Upper World in shamanism.

A person with a strong air element often has great communication skills, quick thinking, and wit. When air is imbalanced, a person may find it hard to adjust to new experiences. They might have a nervous energy, dabble in many ventures, and have a difficult time following through with ideas.

Balancing the Air Element

Balance the air element by focusing on your breath and doing deep belly breathing. There are many forms of breathwork that you can practice. Singing, chanting mantras, and vocal expression also balance the air element. Work with the wind by being outdoors, sensing the quality of the wind, and feeling the breeze on your skin. Use feathers to clear energy on the body and in spaces to balance the air element. Writing and speaking well, being mindful in speech, practicing movement (such as yoga), traveling, and watching birds also connect you to the air element.

» Direction: East

» Season: Spring (autumn in the southern hemisphere)

» Festival: Ostara

» Tools: Feathers, chimes, crystal singing bowl, incense

» Spirits/gods/goddess: Athena, Zeus, sylphs, devas, and faeries

» Zodiac signs: Gemini, Libra, Aquarius

» Planets: Mercury, Jupiter, Uranus

» Chakra: Heart (Anahata)

» Crystals: Citrine, smoky quartz, lapis lazuli

» Herbs: Fennel, lavender, frankincense, sweetgrass

» Colors: Yellow, white, blue

» Mantra: Yam (pronounced "yang")

Air Ceremony

An air ceremony is a shamanic practice that connects you to the spirits of the air element. The spirits of the air element are a living consciousness that is within us through our breath and in our planet's atmosphere. Through ceremony, you can connect with the air elementals and they can be a source of guidance to you.

You can perform an air ceremony anytime you are feeling stuck and rigid. The winds of the air element can assist during times of change and transition. With practice, you will develop a relationship with the spirits of air.

Ceremony

Find a peaceful spot in nature, preferably near trees. Sit quietly, open up sacred space, and call in the Four Directions. Express your intention to connect to the air element, calling in the spirits of the air element with reverence and giving them your heartfelt gratitude.

Imagine roots going down from your root chakra at the base of your spine into the earth. Connect to the earth and feel the earth energy below you.

Take three deep breaths in through your nose and out through your mouth. Continue to pay attention to the sensations of breath going in and out of your nose and into your lungs. Feel your belly rise on the inhale and fall on the exhale.

Feel the air touching your skin. Is there wind or a breeze moving around you? Imagine the wind clearing and cleansing your body of any heavy energy, starting with your head and going down to your feet.

Now pay attention to the quality of the wind: is it loud or is it more of a whisper? Notice whether the wind is moving the leaves in the trees. Observe how the trees are moving with the wind. Contemplate the areas of your life where you too can be more flexible. Send gratitude to the spirits of the air.

Now visualize sending a gold beam of light from your crown chakra at the top of your head to the Upper World. Sense what the higher vibrational energy above you feels like. Is it lighter than the earth energy below you? Do you like how it feels?

Stay in this space for as long as you wish. You can ask a question and see whether any information or insights come to you or simply just be. When you feel you are finished, bring your energy back down to your crown chakra and into your heart chakra. Take a deep breath through the center of your heart.

Give gratitude for everything you learned and experienced, give thanks to the air element, and close the space. You can journal anything that came up for you.

Fire Element

Fire is a masculine element that gives us the energy and will to bring our ideas into manifestation. It is symbolic of transformation, purification, death, and rebirth. Fire helps us transmute lower aspects of ourselves and limiting beliefs into productive energies. The fire element brings light to darkness, burning away our former identity and dissolving our ego. Fire creates and destroys. It represents digestion, personal power, will, passion, vitality, creativity, and courage.

The fire element allows us to purify that which no longer serves us and holds us back from our truest selves; the fire element sets us free. The spirits of the fire teach us how to clear out the old in order to make space for the new to arise. Fire is connected to the phoenix, dragons, and salamanders. Fire governs planning and implementing, inventions, and leaders. In shamanism, fire is thought to help you communicate with the ancestors and spirits.

A person with a strong fire element is passionate, bold, strong, visionary, and focused. Imbalanced fire can show as low self-esteem, recklessness, burnout, depression, anxiety, inflammation, and excessive emotions.

Balancing the Fire Element

Balance the fire element by lighting a candle, gazing into the flame, and asking it to transmute any stuck energies. You can clear negative thought patterns and balance fire energy through meditation, conscious

movement (such as yoga and tai chi), recreational swimming or gentle water exercise, or forms of conscious dance (such as trance dance, conscious dance, 5Rhythms dance). Dancing or praying around fire can help purify stuck energies and connect you back to the spirit in all things. Celebrating life and creating community are also ways of balancing the fire element.

- » Direction: South (north in the southern hemisphere)
- » Season: Summer
- » Festival: Summer solstice (Litha)
- » Tools: Candle, wand, sword
- » Spirits/gods/goddess: Ra, Pele, Sekhmet, Brigid, Hedes, Loki
- » Zodiac signs: Aries, Leo, Sagittarius
- » Planets: Sun, Mars, Jupiter
- » Chakra: Solar plexus (Manipura)
- » Crystals: Obsidian, carnelian, tiger-eye, sunstone
- » Herbs: Angelica, dragon's blood, rosemary, cinnamon
- » Colors: Gold, red, yellow, orange
- » Mantra: Ram (pronounced "rang")

Fire Ceremony

A fire ceremony is a powerful shamanic practice used to release unwanted energies and attachments from the past, making space for new intentions. Use a fire ceremony to release unhappy memories, fears, unhelpful thought patterns, negative emotions, and anything that you are holding on to that doesn't serve your Higher Self. By releasing these unwanted energies and old patterns into the fire, you are healing at the soul level.

You can perform a fire ceremony anytime you feel called to do so or you can also work with the energies during the solstice, equinox, astrological events, or auspicious times, such as the New Year. A fire ceremony can be performed anytime you are feeling stuck, want to create something new, or just feel you need to shift the energy.

Ceremony

Connect with your heart and ask, "What do I need to release? What doesn't serve me anymore?" Gather pictures, create drawings or artwork, and write what you want to release or what intention you want to bring in. Find a burnable offering, sometimes known as a "spirit arrow," that will represent your desired intention, issue, or what you are letting go of.

Prepare a fire using a firepit, fireproof lantern, metal bowl, candle, or barbecue. The fire need not be huge, just make sure that the area is safe for a fire. Have a jug of water or water hose to put the fire out.

Open up sacred space and call in the Four Directions, Mother Earth, and Father Sky. Call in any divine support that you are called to: Spirit, Higher Self, God, Universal Source, spirit helpers, power animals, guardians, and ancestors. You can drum, rattle, and sing, if you choose.

Ask the spirit of the fire to purify you and release what you want to let go of. Ask the spirits of the earth to receive what you are releasing.

Place each item in the fire while you name what you are releasing (you can say it out loud or in your head).

Blow into a stick, with the intention that what you are releasing is going out with your breath, and offer the stick to the fire. If anything else comes up during the ceremony, name it and release it. Place no judgment on what you are releasing.

Thank the fire and put it out. Close the sacred space, give gratitude to the Divine and to the spirits of the elements: earth, wind, fire, and air.

Don't worry about doing it perfectly; it is the intention that matters. Let your intuition guide you. Release any attachment you have to the outcome. When you're in ceremony, you will be surprised at the magick that unfolds.

Water Element

Water is the universal fuel that sustains all of life. Plants, animals, and humans cannot live without water. It is a feminine element of gentle yet immense power that cleanses and heals. Emotions reside in the waves of water, allowing your heart to open with compassion for yourself and others. Dreams, intuition, introspection, fluidity, unconditional love, and psychic abilities are nurtured and guided by water.

The water element is about letting go and freedom. The spirits of the water teach us how to ebb and flow, to be adaptable, and move around bumps in the road with ease. Water is connected to artists, musicians, and the undine and mermaid elementals. Water represents the subconscious mind, the waters of the Earth, love, healing, peace, the womb, and fertility.

A person with a strong water element has a calming energy. They can go with the flow. They are forgiving and have a healthy emotional body. With an imbalance in water, a person can be detached, fearful, overly emotional, and lack boundaries.

Balancing the Water Element

Balance the water element by observing a body of water: lake, stream, ocean, or waterfall. As you observe the water, contemplate how you can create more flow in your life. Listen to music with the sound of flowing water. Make a water despacho (see page 156). Say your prayers into a cup or chalice of water and put it on your altar or you can drink it.

» Direction: West

» Season: Autumn (spring in the southern hemisphere)

» Festival: Mabon (autumnal equinox)

» Tools: Chalice, bowl, cauldron, abalone shell

» Spirits/gods/goddess: Isis, Mary, Aphrodite, Yemaya, Osiris,

» Zodiac signs: Cancer, Scorpio, Pisces

» Planets: Moon, Venus, Neptune

» Chakra: Sacral (Swadhisthana)

» Crystals: Moonstone, selenite, amazonite, rose quartz

» Herbs: Chamomile, mugwort, rose

» Colors: Blue, green, turquoise

» Mantra: Vam (pronounced as "vang")

Water Ceremony

The waters of the ocean are always in motion, ebbing and flowing. The ocean can be calm or aggressive. The tides rise and fall, letting the motion come and go. Just like the ocean, when the water element is balanced, you will allow emotions to arise naturally and pass through you. If you cannot process your emotions and if you are having difficulty going with the flow, your emotional state will be unstable. Your water element is out of balance.

You can consciously balance your water element through ceremony, invoking the water element into your day by being near a body of water and watching how the water flows effortlessly. As the water element comes back into balance, you will find it easier to surrender, allowing for the flow of life's events.

Immersing yourself in water by taking a ceremonial bath is a wonderful way to align yourself with the water element. This is a bath taken for a spiritual purpose with a specific intention. A water ceremony is relaxing, cleansing, and purifying, and connects you to Spirit. Ritual baths can be used for a plethora of intentions and what you add to the bath brings more magick, power, and depth. For more potency, you can perform your ritual baths with auspicious dates.

Ceremony

To use essential oils, crystals, herbs, and flowers, do your research ahead of time to ensure they are safe and can be immersed in water. Do a test spot with the essential oil on your skin and check compatibilities if you plan to use multiple oils. If you plan to use herbs, add infused water to the bath. (Steeping and straining the infusion makes for an easy cleanup afterward). You can also add herbs to a tea bag and let that steep in your water. If you use rose petals and flowers, it is nice to put them directly in the bath. Have fun selecting what you will bring!

Begin by asking yourself what the purpose is for the bath ceremony. Is there something specific you want to release or receive guidance on? Gather items that align with your intention for the bath. Some suggestions are roses, crystals, essential oils, herbs, a cup of Epsom salts, candles, a lighter, sage, a shell or cauldron, music, and healing waters collected from sacred sites.

Run the bath and light candles. Smudge yourself and the space with sage or an herb of your choice.

Open up sacred space by calling in the Four Directions, Mother Earth, and Father Sky. Call in any divine support that you feel you need: Spirit, Higher Self, Creator, God, Universal Source, spirit helpers, power animals, guardians, and ancestors. Call in the water element and state your intention for the bath ritual. It could simply be to connect to the water element, to bring more water and flow into your life.

Spread the rose petals (if using) in the bath, and offer each petal to the water with love and gratitude. Add the essential oils and salt (if using) for clearing. Crystals that will not dissolve in water can be added or left on the side of the tub.

Get in the tub and allow yourself to be immersed in the energy and beautiful fragrances. Feel and imagine the water cleansing your energy field and dissolving away anything that isn't serving you.

Allow yourself to surrender to the ebb and flow of the water. Let the rose petals wash over you. Visualize, feel, and become immersed in your intention. How would it feel if you already had your intention? See yourself with that intention in your third eye.

When you feel lighter, energized, and complete with the ritual, give thanks and close the space.

Earth Element

The Earth provides us with a home, stability, protection, and nurturing. It's the foundation of our existence. Mother Earth is the womb from which all of life emerges and the home of the plant, mineral, and animal kingdoms. The earth element represents strength, abundance, wealth, prosperity, and health. This is the realm where we manifest everything into our reality. To succeed in life, whether that is in business, health, or relationships, we need a solid anchor to connect us to Source Energy, the wellspring from which life is created. Earth is that anchor.

Earth is a feminine element that nurtures and protects us, representing the middle world in shamanism. Earth is connected to the gnomes and nature spirits. It is the home and foundation for our physical bodies, and our physical bodies are the home for our spirit. Here we experience the cycles of life: growth, destruction, death, and rebirth. Strongly connecting to the earth element gives us compassion for all of life, allowing us to embody our spirit and trust in our journey and giving us the gift of manifesting our highest potential.

The earth element provides us with nature, giving us one of our greatest ways to heal. The earth absorbs and transforms our stress and heavy energy. Our earth is magnetic and is able to clear and charge our energy field.

A person who is grateful, patient, solid, stable, and reliable has a strong earth element. An imbalance in earth results in excessive worry, lack of self-care, and lack of nurturing.

Balancing the Earth Element

Balance the earth element by nurturing yourself. For example, indulge in a massage, spend time in nature, hike in the mountains, or garden. Walk on the ground barefoot. Give gratitude for the blessings in your life. Engage in embodiment practices through exercise, yoga, dance, or 5Rhythms. Eat grounding foods, such as root vegetables, or enjoy a piece of cacao.

» Direction: North (south in the southern hemisphere)

» Season: Winter

- » Festival: Yule (winter solstice)
- » Tools: Salt, crystals, stones
- » Spirits/gods/goddess: Gaia, Pachamama, nature spirits
- » Zodiac signs: Taurus, Virgo, Capricorn
- » Planet: Saturn, Venus, Mercury
- » Chakra: Root (Muladhara)
- » Crystals: Black tourmaline, shungite, malachite
- » Herbs: Vetiver, myrrh, wormwood
- » Colors: Green, black, brown, yellow
- » Mantra: Lam (pronounced as "lang")

Earth Ceremony

This is a walking meditation ceremony that will involve walking barefoot in nature. You will need to find a safe place you can stroll barefoot. It can be in your backyard, on a beach, or in a park. Earthing, also known as grounding, refers to creating a physical connection in between the electrical magnetic frequencies of the earth and the human body. Studies have shown that the subtle energies of the earth have numerous health benefits. Note that 20 to 30 minutes of physical connection to the earth is needed to reap the full benefits; however, any amount of time can be beneficial.

Ceremony

Open up sacred space and call in the Four Directions, Mother Earth, and Father Sky. Call in any divine support that you feel you need: Spirit, Higher Self, God, Creator, Universal Source, spirit helpers, power animals, guardians, and ancestors. State your intention for the ceremony: to connect to Mother Earth, transmute any heavy energies in your body, receive any messages you need, and give gratitude to the Earth for all that she provides you.

Begin to slowly walk barefoot by taking mindful steps—press your left foot, then your right foot, into the ground. Feel the earth beneath your feet. Take your time to engage every part of your foot slowly (the heel, the ball of your foot, and each toe) as it makes contact with the ground.

Be aware of all the sensations in your feet. If there is moisture on the grass or it feels dry, take a moment to absorb the sensation into your body. Engage in your sense of smell—does the earth have a particular scent you recognize?

Become immersed in each moment by observing all the sensations that arise. If thoughts arise, simply let them pass by and continue to focus on the experience.

Now focus on the physical sensations in your body where you have tightness or heavy energy. Send those energies through your feet and into the earth. Ask Mother Earth to transmute those energies and give gratitude to her, then feel any heaviness drain from your feet.

As you continue to walk slowly, think of all the earthly pleasures you are grateful for. Thank the Earth for as many things as you can think of. Feel the gratitude in your heart chakra.

Ask whether there are any messages for you or ask a specific question. Observe everything around you; nature has a magickal way of providing messages when you are open to receiving them. If you see any animals, you can look up their symbolic meaning.

When you feel complete, you can finish your walk and close the space. Notice how you feel and journal anything that might have come up for you.

Akasha

Akasha is the Sanskrit word for Aether, Space, and Spirit. It is the eternal field in which everything happens. The physical reality you experience occurs in Akasha. Akasha is formless. It is the matrix that is the source of all matter and simultaneously the space in which it exists. All the other elements arise from the primal source energy of Akasha.

Akasha cannot be seen. It is characterized as a vibration and perceived as sound. It is able to permeate everything and yet we cannot touch it. Akasha holds the consciousness of all living things, including plants and animals. Consciousness is your awareness of your internal and external existence and your ability to experience life.

The throat chakra is connected to Akasha: your throat chakra is the place where vibration is expressed as sound. When you listen to uplifting sounds, you are accessing a gateway to the Akashic realm. When you get quiet and go within, you are connecting to the space of Akasha. When you are in ceremony and prayer, you are entering into the field of Akasha, the space of infinite possibilities and divine mystery.

Akasha is known as the Creator of all things, bringing everything into being. This is where you create and manifest what you want to bring into your life. Entering into the space of Akasha is the first step in bringing what you want into being. You will know you have entered into the field of Akasha when you feel a deep sense of peace and bliss. Akasha opens the doorway to your soul, to your divinity.

An imbalance in Akasha will show as someone who is unable to slow down and be still. It can also manifest as issues around the throat chakra, as an inability to express oneself and speak one's truth.

Balancing Akasha

To balance Akasha, listen to sounds, such as crystal singing bowls, Balinese bells, and Koshi chimes. Play instruments, chant mantras, and sing. Feel the subtle space around your body. Practice yoga, bringing your awareness to the space around you and simultaneously to your breath. Take breaks from technology and be still. Go into nature and connect to everything around you. Sit in meditation and prayer.

» Direction: Everywhere, all directions, center

» Tools: Divination, all tools

» Spirits/gods/goddess: All

» Zodiac signs: no signs

» Chakra: Throat (Vishuddha)

» Crystals: Amethyst, moldavite, andara

» Herbs: Lavender, frankincense, geranium

» Colors: White, platinum silver, black

» Mantra: Ham (pronounced "hang")

Akasha Ceremony

Akasha or Spirit is around you and within you at all times. You can connect to the infinite field of akasha at any time that you are feeling off center, emotional, stressed, or have too much mental chatter. Connecting to akasha allows you to bring your focus off the small details of your life and into the bigger picture. You enter into the zero point energy field where you feel love, peace, balance, stillness and limitless possibilities.

Find a private and peaceful space. Smudge with sage and open up sacred space. Call in the directions. Play some light ambient music in the background, or use singing bowls, chimes, or bells.

State your intention to connect to the Akashic field. Take three deep breaths in through your nose and out through your mouth. Imagine roots going down from your root chakra at the base of your spine into the earth. Connect to the earth and feel the earth energy below you, feeling grounded to Mother Earth. Release any heaviness you may feel into the earth.

Visualize a blue swirling light in your throat chakra; imagine this light is cleansing and clearing your throat chakra. Now vocal tone the Sanskrit mantra Ham, pronounced "hang," on the exhale, in the back of the throat. Continue to repeat the mantra for 5 minutes and feel the vibration in your throat chakra and body.

Now just be still with your eyes closed. Allow yourself to feel the emptiness. Let go of any judgments or preconceived notions about how you should think or feel. Continue to focus on the sounds and the space around you with an impartial and compassionate view. When you notice thoughts arise, simply allow them to pass and bring your attention back to the sounds and space.

Allow whatever arises for you to come up. Note any visualizations, guidance, or insights you receive. Ask questions out loud or in your head. You may receive the answer in a feeling, a voice, a visualization, or a sense of knowing. If nothing comes, just sit with that presence and allow it to pass through.

Enjoy the loving embrace of the Akashic field as long as you wish. Give gratitude for everything that you received.

Invocation of the Five Elements

You can harness the energies of the five elements in your life for personal power and balance. Call them into your daily life through prayer, by honoring their energies, and by inviting them to guide you. Do this invocation daily and you will develop a deep connection with the elements.

This invocation can be done in nature or at your altar space (see page 68). You will have an offering for each element. You can choose an offering that feels right for you. As a suggestion, you can use a quartz crystal for Akasha, a lit candle for the fire element, an incense stick for the air element, a glass of water for the water element, and salt for the earth element.

You will find your own words for this invocation. Or call on all the elements or individual elements if you only need their specific energies and characteristics.

Ceremony

With a quartz crystal in your hand, say out loud: "I call to Akasha, the great mystery, bring me your wisdom. I invite you into my life. Teach me all the ways to create and manifest my highest good. I honor you."

Now on your next exhale, breath your prayer into the crystal.

Light the candle and while gazing into the flame and say: "I call the fire element into my life and body. I honor your transformative energies and I invite them into my life to illuminate my path. I ask the fire to help me purify, transmute and transform the

aspects of myself and my life that no longer serve me."

Now light the incense and let the smoke blow over you, your space or altar. Say: "I call to the air element and I invite you into this space. I ask the powers of air to teach me how to accept movement and change in my life. Help me to connect to my Higher Self and the spirits of the winds. Be here with me, I honor you, and thank you."

Now pick up your glass of water and speak into your cup of water: "I call to the water element, infuse my life with the ability to go with the flow. I ask you to cleanse any heaviness from by body, emotions and spirit. Please help me surrender to the natural flow of life with ease and grace." If you are outdoors, you can offer the water back into the earth or you can do it when you are finished with the invocation.

Next, take your salt and offer it to the soil or ground outside and say: "I call to the earth element, bring your energies of stability and trust into my life. Teach me how to feel anchored and grounded to the earth. I ask for your protection. Thank you, and so it is, Aho."

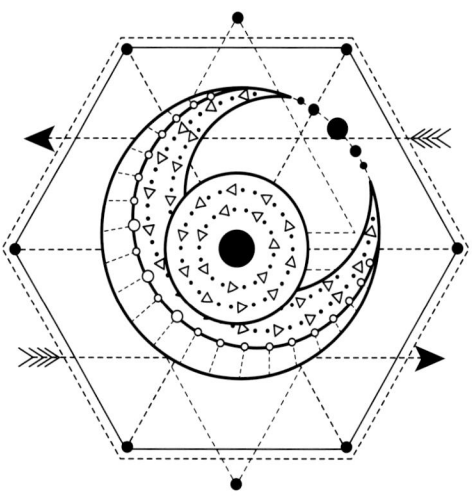

07
The Crystal and Mineral Kingdom

Stones and crystals are very much alive and conscious, and they are considered sacred and healing allies to a shaman. Stones and crystals are highly evolved tools used in protection, shamanic journeying, divination, inner work, and healing the energy body. Many stones carry "programs" or "codes" of information inside of them because they have witnessed the passing of the ages. Everything from a severe weather event to a ritual ceremony to a catastrophic explosion— the stones have seen it all.

Through these experiences, they have acquired wisdom, and so can be of great assistance to us. Although they don't seem to communicate in the way plants or animals do, make no mistake: they are just as powerful and carry great medicine if we learn how to use them appropriately.

Some stones are very beautiful to the eye, but they are not just worn as adornment or as fashion—stone medicine has been an integral part of many ancient civilizations for centuries. Every ancient culture, from Greece and Rome to Egypt and China, has used crystals for various purposes. These include everything from fashioning weapons and tools (flint or obsidian), to wearing protective amulets (jade or ruby), to crushing fine pigments to use as makeup (lapis lazuli). Many ancient sites were chosen because of their proximity to stones—think of Stonehenge, Sedona, and Machu Picchu. The ancient medicine people knew how to harness and maximize the energetic vortices of these specific places to maintain stability and harmony in the land where they lived. Certain groups, such as the shamans in the Andes, are known as pioneers in stone medicine. They infuse them with the highest energies through their breath and honor the high mountains where their stones came from. The Australian Aborigines also used quartz crystals in their initiation rituals and used them to ignite their highest potential.

In modern times, crystals are at the core of everything we do—your computer and smartphone would not function without quartz crystals. They are found in medical devices, tools, airplanes, and automobiles. Because of their inherently balanced nature, crystals are used in multiple ways to store, emit, and transform frequency and information.

How Crystals Work

Crystals have formed over millions, sometimes billions, of years inside the Earth's crust. They carry memory and everything that has passed on this planet. These incredible stones have been exposed to extreme temperature and pressure, coming out of the surface to support humankind with our ascension. Stones and crystals can help us heal on all physical, emotional, mental, and spiritual levels.

Crystal healing involves placing specific types of crystals either close to the body's energetic field or directly on our skin. This helps bring our bodies back into balance. It works because crystals have a perfect molecular and geometric structure. They are highly stable, organized in repetitive patterns and shapes at an atomic level. The law of entrainment, or the law of resonance, states that the object with a lower frequency will naturally entrain—meaning to incorporate or become a natural part of—toward the object with a higher dominating frequency. This means that if the human body and energy field, which is more disorganized and operating at a lower frequency, comes into contact with a crystal, then the body will naturally gravitate toward the higher frequency object—the crystal.

Crystal healing acts at the level of vibration and harnesses the power of resonant energy. Shamans know how to direct specific stones and work with their energies to bring alignment to the person who needs healing. They develop relationships with their stones and the spirits within them, as they do with all of their allies, to listen to their messages and bring forth their wisdom and healing potential.

How Shamans Use Crystals and Stones

You will likely see some kind or stone or crystal inside every shaman's medicine kit or bundle. Shamans use their crystal helpers to either move stagnant or heavy energy out of a person's energetic field or transform it into a more organized form. A common way to do this is to use a crystal wand or rod as a conduit to redirect the heavy energy out of a person's auric field and neutralize it.

Shamans also commonly use a stone for extracting negative energies and entities from a person's subtle energy body. They can either allow the entity to be absorbed into the stone itself, or they can use the stone as a tool to remove it from a person's aura and redirect it back into Mother Earth. Some shamans incorporate breathing techniques to help move the energy in and out of the stones. They learn to connect their breath to the energy of the crystal to facilitate the healing process.

Other healing methods include placing crystals in a specific grid pattern or layout, depending on what needs to be healed. For a heart chakra wound, a shaman may place a group of stones around the heart center, bringing it back into coherence. Or they may select certain crystals around the head/scalp region, if a person has mental challenges, headaches, or suffers from overthinking.

Shamans may also look to garner information

COMMON STONES USED FOR SHAMANIC PRACTICE

Crystals can pack a big punch—they are used for multiple purposes, such as energy healing, attracting relationships, and strengthening spiritual connections. Below is a list of common crystals you can use to begin your own medicine bundle.

CLEAR QUARTZ: This is one of the most abundant minerals on Earth. Many shamanic traditions consider this the "master stone," as it can amplify energy. It is also piezoelectric, which means you can flow electricity through quartz when you apply mechanical energy or pressure to it.

ROSE QUARTZ: This is the quintessential stone for healing the heart, self-love, compassion, or attracting love into your life. Its energy is very gentle and nurturing, supportive of all.

BLACK TOURMALINE: This is a very grounding and protective stone. Black tourmaline is ideal for transmuting negative energies and a good choice to use around the home or in your workplace. It can help cleanse "bad vibes" and regulate our energy system to reduce stress and worry.

SHUNGITE: A stone for protection from unwanted energies and harmful EMFs from Wi-Fi and electronics, shungite supports clearing out old mental and emotional programs that no longer support you, making way for new and beneficial ways of being.

AMETHYST: This beautiful purple crystal helps with psychic vision. It opens the third eye and facilitates meditative practices and spiritual purification. It also enhances the physical home or work environment by surrounding it in a bubble of light.

SELENITE: An angelic, cleansing stone, selenite is useful in every shaman's arsenal. It restores balance and calm to a person's energy field. Use a stick of selenite and run it over your own body or someone else's.

ANY STONE IN NATURE: One of the best stone allies you will find is right in your own neighborhood. Go for a stroll in a nearby park or natural area and see whether a stone calls out to you. Not all rocks need to be glamorous or flashy, but they still carry wisdom.

or wisdom from the stone itself. A crystal may help the shaman reach an altered state or journey into other realms. Crystals can communicate with us and convey messages. Shamans are able to receive and interpret their messages, because they do not see a rock or a stone as separate from themselves.

Everyday Uses for Crystals

Crystals can be useful companions and friends in all situations. You can carry a crystal in your pocket or purse, place it on your desk at work, or even carry one in your suitcase when you travel. Carry a black stone, such as black tourmaline or obsidian, in your pocket and it will absorb any unwanted energies from the environment you are in. Crystals can also help elevate the energy of a home. Try placing a rose quartz or an amethyst tower in a prominent place in your living room or bedroom. Wearing jewelry on your hands or feet or around your neck is another easy way to incorporate crystals into your everyday routine.

Crystals are also highly programmable, because of their ability to store and amplify energy. You can infuse your intention into a stone as a shaman might do, by asking it to help you with a higher purpose. For example, tiger-eye is a quartz crystal that can help with mental focus and acuity—you may ask the stone to help you during a job interview or an exam. Tiger-eye or kunzite is also a very helpful travel companion—keep a small tumbled stone in your carry-on or suitcase for a safe and smooth journey. You can also create simple crystal grids around your office or bedroom by placing a stone such as black tourmaline or amethyst in each corner of the room for protection and comfort.

No matter how you use them, crystals and stones can raise your vibration and bring your body back into balance. Always be sure to purchase your crystals mindfully from a trusted source.

Ceremony: Learn How to Speak the Language of Crystals

This exercise will help you connect with your stones and build a relationship with them. When selecting stones, always choose the ones you naturally gravitate toward first. Do not be tempted to select the prettiest, smoothest, or largest stone—it is the energy signature and vibration you are looking for. Usually, the first stone you see or pick up is the one for you. Once you have selected your stone, you may wish to cleanse it either by running it under some water (if appropriate), wiping it with a cloth, using a singing bowl, or offering some sage or palo santo smoke to purify it.

Find a quiet place where you will be undisturbed. You may wish to light a candle as you enter into meditation with your chosen crystal.

Observe the crystal closely: note its color, shape, size, and texture. Hold it in the palm of your hand and see if you can feel the energy emanating from it—is it cold, warm, tingly?

Relax your body and focus on your breath. Holding the crystal either in your hands or close to your body near a chakra (e.g., on the heart, stomach or forehead), clear your mind and intend to forge a connection with the crystal. Be open-minded and understand that crystals communicate at the level of vibration and invisible frequency, not with the five senses.

Spend 10 to 15 minutes in quiet meditation with your stone and be aware of any feelings, sensations, or emotions that arise when working with it. If you are open and clear, you may receive messages and information from your crystal.

When you are finished, place your crystal in a safe spot and be sure to leave it under the sunlight (depending on the stone) for cleansing and energising. Write in your journal what you have experienced with your crystal.

Cleansing and Charging Crystals

Crystals store and amplify energies and it is important to cleanse them regularly so they will continue to have a high vibration and work the way you intend them to. Because crystals store energies, you can also program them for specific intentions.

To cleanse your crystals, use sunshine, sage, the earth, salt water, or fresh stream water. To charge your crystals use sunshine or energy healing.

To program your crystals, clear your mind and move your awareness into your heart space. Set your intentions in accordance with the properties of the stone and what energies you want to bring into your life (e.g., a loving relationship). You can hold your crystal up to your heart and imagine the crystal being infused with your intention. Speak your intention out loud or in your head, such as "I have a loving relationship." You can also blow your intentions into the crystal while holding the stone. Do this until you feel the crystal has been programmed.

08
Plant Spirit Healing

Plants have been used in the daily life of every culture in the world. Shamans have always seen themselves as part of nature, and this connection allowed them to communicate with plants. Dating to the Stone Age, shamans have used plants, oils, and herbs to shift consciousness, heal, and connect to the spirit world. The ancients knew that the plants were healers and teachers with a consciousness and spirit of their own. The plant spirits were allies who helped them bring harmony, balance, and healing to those they served.

Plants will reconnect you with the sacredness of our Earth and the natural world. And using plants is available to us all—Mother Earth provides us the most powerful medicine cabinet. Each plant has its own unique frequency and offers its own specific knowledge and healing. Plants have been used to heal everything from cuts and wounds to diseases and illnesses to emotional and spiritual imbalances. Through experiments and with guidance from the plants, the ancients learned to combine certain plants into mixtures for specific outcomes. When the spirit of the plant connects to our physical Humanness, it shows us the sacredness of the spirit in all things.

The plant spirits teach us to anchor the above and below into this physical plane. They clear congestion from our hearts, energy field, and spaces so we can operate from our highest good without outside influences. But just as humans are all unique with our own consciousness, so are plants. This means they may function and benefit differently for different people. You will develop your own individual relationships with the plant spirits, and they will function in a way that is specific to you. While plants have common and agreed-upon benefits, this can vary from person to person. Exploring different plants and learning what gifts they bring you and

what they have to teach you is a powerful practice.

NOTE: Take care when selecting and purchasing herbs, oils, and plants. Be mindful of where they come from, so you receive the most benefit from them and also care for the environment.

Sacred Oils and Scents

Of all our senses—touch, taste, smell, and sight—our sense of smell is the only sense that is a direct portal into our soul and unconscious. All the other senses are filtered through the thalamus (part of the brain stem). This means that what is sensed is modulated by the brain before entering into your conscious awareness. When you smell an aroma, the scent goes directly to your limbic system, which is responsible for emotions and memory. This is how aromas can uplift your mood and calm emotions.

Shamans, healers, and medicine men and women have used essential oils for physical, emotional, and mental healing. These are the aromatic substances extracted from a plant, such as frankincense. Essential oils are seventy-five to a hundred times stronger than the dried plant. The highly concentrated oils contain the essence (spirit) of the plant and have many beneficial uses. The benefits of essential oils can be experienced through the nose and the skin on the body, face, soles of our feet, and palms of our hands.

NOTE: Certain essential oils can irritate the skin.

Always do a spot test with a new oil. As a general guideline, it is best to dilute essential oils used on the skin with a carrier oil, such as jojoba or almond oil. There are many options for carrier oils. Not all essential oils blend well together. Check before blending oils.

When you smell an essential oil, connect to the spirit of that plant. You can do this by putting a few drops of oil in your hands—be sure to check whether the oil needs to be diluted with a carrier oil first. Next, cup your hands and bring them to cover your mouth and nose. Inhale the scent and simultaneously connect to the spirit of the plant by visualizing it in its natural environment or repeating its name while focusing on its essence. As you connect to the spirit of the essential oil you bring its vibration into your energy field. You will find the use of any plant more powerful when you connect to the spirit of it.

Anointing with sacred oils has been performed in a ceremonial way for thousands of years. Mary Magdalene is associated with the sacred act of anointing with oils, and she also anointed Yeshua's feet with sacred oils as an act of worship, healing, and appreciation. Anointing is symbolic of blessing, love, honor, and protection.

Essential Oil Blends

Essential oils can be used individually or blended and used during your healing work and ceremonies. You can combine oils to achieve the energies and benefits you desire (e.g., protection, abundance, calming, and energizing).

Essential oils can be used all over the body. For example, peppermint on the temples and forehead is a great remedy for a headache. Oils can be used for muscle soreness or along the chakras of the body and on the face in skin care. One of the most highly absorbable areas to place oils is on the soles of your feet and the palms of your hands.

COMMON ESSENTIAL OILS

Angelica: calming, soothing, relaxing

Bergamot: uplifting, balances emotions, energizing

Black pepper: promotes courage, expansion, protection

Birch: activating, cleansing, soothing

Cedarwood: calming, protection, enhances spirituality

Chamomile: relaxing, peacefulness, meditation

Cypress: invigorating, blessings, protection

Fir: cleansing, renewing, uplifting

Frankincense: grounding, spiritual activation, protection

Jasmine: joy, peace, confidence

Juniper berry: purification, cleansing, invigorating

Lavender: balancing, refreshing, calming

Neroli: happiness, purification, calming

Pine: new beginnings, protection, regeneration

Rose: love, peace, beauty (highest vibration of all oils)

Rosemary: clarity, stimulating, cleansing

Sandalwood: spirituality, meditation, sexuality

Spruce: grounding, emotional release, love

Vetiver: abundance, regenerating, grounding

Ylang-ylang: peace, love, sensuality

Essential Oil Recipe

This essential oil blend cleanses and protects your body and aura from outside influences. The blend can be prepared in three different ways: for a diffuser, as a body oil, or as a spray (as a replacement for smudging).

Use the diffuser to clear your home and space. Use the body oil along your chakras and on the back of the neck, the low back, the palms, and the feet. Use the spray whenever you feel heavy energy on your body and in any space.

Essential Oils
Cedar 2–3 drops per 10 ml
Frankincense 2–3 drops per 10 ml
Palo santo 2–3 drops per 10 ml
Lavender 2–3 drops per 10 ml

For Diffuser
5- or 10-ml bottle

For Body Oil
Jojoba carrier oil 90 ml
Small bowl or container ~ 100 ml

For Spray
Purified water 80 ml
Witch hazel 1 tablespoon
Spray bottle 100 ml bottle

Feel free to omit or use less or more of the ingredients, to what suits you.

For the diffuser: Combine the cedar, frankincense, palo santo, and lavender oils in a small bottle and shake to blend. Place 5-10 drops of the mix in a diffuser.

For the body oil: Combine the cedar, frankincense, palo santo, and lavender oils with the jojoba oil in a small container and shake to blend.

For the spray: Combine the cedar, frankincense, palo santo, and lavender oils in a spray bottle, add the water and witch hazel, and shake to blend.

Sacred Smoke

The fire element taught our ancestors about the cycles of life and that burning dried plants—herbs, roots, bark, and resins—would produce smoke. As the plants transition from their physical form (from the fire), they transform into smoke, entering the world of spirit. Thus, the smoke brings us a connection to the spirit realm.

Incense

The sacred smoke from burning incense has been used in many shamanic traditions as a symbol of prayer and offering to the Divine. Incense can be used in ceremony and meditation, and to create sacred space, uplift, or cleanse the energy in a space.

Incense comes in the form of cones, sticks, and resins. Use an incense burner. If you don't have one, a ceramic bowl or any fireproof container will work. Light the incense and let it burn for a few seconds, then blow out the flame. There should be a red tip and it will smoke. You might need to place the incense near a window or on a higher shelf if the scent and smoke are too overpowering. Enjoy the smell. Scents have such a profound effect on our well-being.

Varieties of Incense

There are endless varieties of incense to choose from, all invoking different qualities and benefits. Here are a few you can start with:

Calming Fragrances

» Relax with frankincense, sandalwood, and cedarwood.

» Reduce stress with sandalwood, lavender, and rosemary.

» Get better sleep with lavender, vetiver, and chamomile.

» Meditate with sandalwood and lotus.

Stimulating Fragrances

» Cleanse your space and power objects with cedar, myrrh, or citrus.

» Focus and concentrate with sandalwood.

» Create with lemongrass, citrus, geranium, and ylang-ylang.

» Encourage psychic abilities and visions with frankincense and cedarwood.

Smudging and Blessing

Smudging with sacred smoke from the burning of plants and herbs has traditionally been used by Native Americans and many other cultures. Smudging is generally a ceremony used to cleanse and purify unwanted energy from a person, place, or object and to call in blessings and healing. Various sacred plants are used, such as tobacco, sage, sweetgrass, cedar, lavender, and juniper, depending on the desired outcome and the method of smudging. The spirits of the plants are then called to assist. Burning the herbs inside a shell combines all four elements: the herbs as the earth element, the shell as the water element, the flame as fire element, and the smoke representing the air element. Plant spirits are wise and like to be treated with respect in order to reap their healing benefits.

Sacred Herbs

SAGE: Use white sage *Salvia apiana* for cleansing and purifying unwanted energies from your energetic field and body, home, business, car, and any object. Smudge with sage after your workday to clear any energies you might have picked up from others. Clear your home after you have an argument with a loved one and after you have houseguests. When you are feeling off or stressed, smudging with sage can lighten things up. Clearing with sage feels like taking a breath of fresh air.

Intentions: I release any heavy energies. I let go of anything that no longer serves my highest good.

PALO SANTO: The use of palo santo (*Bursera graveolens*), a tree native to South America, traces back to the Incan empire. Also known as holy wood, this aromatic stick is used for cleansing and purifying energy, blessing, bringing in positive energy, and promoting relaxation. Using palo santo can help you feel more grounded and bring clarity to a situation. The palo santo tree must die naturally and be left for three years before it is properly harvested. Palo santo is another great travel ally to cleanse and uplift the vibration of new spaces.

Use palo santo in a similar way as smudging with sage: Light the stick; it usually needs to burn for a few moments until you see a red tip. Gently blow the flame out and follow the smudging steps. You might need to relight the stick if the smoke goes out. Be mindful of the source of your herbs to ensure the harvesting is ethical and sustainable.

Intentions: I purify this space with the highest vibration. I bless this space with joy, love, and peace. I call in the energies of abundance.

TOBACCO: The traditional use of tobacco (*Nicotiana rustica*) has a rich history, and it is considered one of the most sacred plants. Tobacco was used to communicate and send prayers to the spirit world, often through the sacred pipe or *chanupa* (see page 161). Tobacco has been an essential part of shamanic ceremony and is often used for protection, purification, and healing. Tobacco can also be used for offerings to elders and shamans.

The tobacco spirit has so much to teach but is often exploited. Nicotine is the addictive component of all tobacco. There is no doubt that commercial tobacco has added dangerous chemicals, but even pure tobacco can become addictive. Use tobacco with respect and in a ceremonial way, not to escape or mask emotions. It is best to use the purest form of tobacco with no additional ingredients.

Tobacco comes in many forms and there are many ways to use it. You can purchase loose cigarette or pipe tobacco at a store. Tobacco can be smoked, burned, or chewed. Powdered tobacco mixed with other sacred herbs is known as rapé, or shamanic snuff. Mapacho tobacco is used by the shamans in South America and has a high nicotine content.

Intentions: I am centered and grounded. I am cleansed and purified of lower energies.

CEDAR: Cedar is a sacred medicine, as cedar trees are very wise and powerful spirits. Its smoke is used for clearing energy, purification, healing, and protection. Cedar use is also associated with strength, blessing, offerings, and prayers. Cedar can be used for smudging and is often used to cleanse unwanted energies from new homes. Loose herbs are put into the fire during ceremony.

Intentions: This space is cleansed, purified, and protected. I offer this cedar to the spirits of this land.

How to Smudge

There are many ways to smudge and there is no right or wrong way. What is important is the intention behind the smudging ceremony.

» Sage or another herb

» Shell, ceramic bowl, or other fireproof bowl

» Lighter

» Feather

Open a door or window to let the smoke out if you are indoors. Call in any helping spirits and the spirit of the plant you are using. Remember that your intention is key.

Place dried sage leaves in a shell or bowl. Hold your intention in your thoughts for a minute or two (cleansing negative or unwanted energies, bringing positivity, removing doubts, eliminating negative thoughts, etc.).

Light the sage while holding your intention. Let it burn for about 30 seconds, then carefully blow out the flame.

Use a feather to fan the smoke over your body (or someone else's body), starting above the head and slowly moving down the body to the bottom of the feet, covering all your chakras. Don't forget about your hands and under your feet.

To smudge a home or space, walk around the perimeter of the space while fanning the smoke with the feather. Get into all corners. Open a window and allow the smoke to blow out as it carries the unwanted energies.

Discard of the ashes by returning them to the earth. Don't forget to give thanks and express gratitude.

Part III
THE WAY OF
THE SHAMAN

09
Shamanic Space
Clearing and Blessing

Just as our chakras and our aura accumulate energies, so do our personal spaces. Energy stagnates in the spaces we inhabit—our homes, businesses, cars, and land. When we don't clear these spaces, heavy energies accumulate, affecting our well-being, health, emotions, and relationships. When the energy of our space doesn't align with what we are trying to achieve, we often feel stuck, depressed, unmotivated, stressed, and blocked.

As energetic beings, we are deeply affected by the spaces that we are in. Our homes are our temples. It is very empowering when you discover that you can shift your inner and outer world by clearing your physical spaces through the sacred ceremony of space clearing. When the stagnant energies are cleared, you will feel increased happiness, joy, and love. You will notice you are more productive; you sleep better and your relationships and finances improve. All areas of your life will shift when you shift the energy in your space.

Why Do We Need to Space Clear?

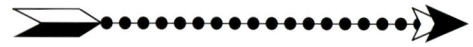

Sometimes we are feeling stuck, sluggish, and heavy, and we don't realize why. We might think how we are feeling is something within us when it is actually our environment. We rarely associate our productivity and happiness with our homes, workplaces, or the buildings we enter.

Space clearing is an ancient practice that was a way of life for shamans and many cultures around the world. This tradition was important to our ancestors because they understood that everything is alive and connected. They wanted to keep harmony in their personal environments and lives. Space clearing purifies and balances the energies and creates an openness to bring in higher vibrational energy and blessings.

As energetic beings, we are constantly shifting and moving our energy—inadvertently, we deposit energy in the spaces we inhabit. The energy we leave behind accumulates and turns into energetic sludge. This unwanted energy builds up along the walls and in the corners of rooms. After a space-clearing ceremony, the space always looks bigger because when the built-up energy is released, the space can open up.

When you move into a new home or office, the residual energy of the previous inhabitants will remain in the space. Everything that occurred there has left its imprint. When you immerse yourself in the energies left behind, they affect you. For example, if there was someone with a severe illness in the home before you, you might notice your health decline. There could have been fighting, divorce, death, financial loss, and so on, that could have occurred as far back as the place exists. Even if it is good energy left behind, you want to start off with a clean slate. When you move to a new home or office, it is a new beginning and you want a fresh start. You need not take on any energies that were left behind.

Another important aspect of space clearing is clearing clutter. Just as clutter piles up, so does the energy around it. You can't do a proper space clearing without clearing clutter first. It is like trying to mow the lawn without a lawn mower—the grass will not be cut properly. Clutter contains the energy imprints from the past and from wherever it was before. It piles up and distorts the space with things you don't need, use, or care about anymore. Along with clutter

comes an accumulation of energies you don't need. When you clear clutter and energy, you make space for the new to come in through your intentions.

Why Do We Need to Bless a Space?

Blessing the space is often done after the energies have been broken up and released. Once the space is cleared, the energies you wish to call in can be invoked through intention and prayers.

You can bless as space for virtually anything that you desire to bring into your life, such as love, prosperity, happiness, good health, abundance, financial wealth, success, spiritual growth and peace. When you bless your space, you call in the assistance from the higher realms—your team of spiritual helpers. With this supernatural support and divine energy, you can achieve miraculous things.

Space-Clearing Tools

There are a variety tools that can clear and bless spaces. Space-clearing tools from our ancient past are still just as powerful and used today (e.g., herbs, drums, rattles, bells, sacred herbs, and oils). Others are more modern, such as singing bowls and crystal wands. Regardless of what tools are used, it is vital to align with spirit, intention, and gratitude.

How do you know what to use to clear your space? There are certain tools that are more effective for specific tasks. Clearing and blessing require different processes and tools.

GOOD TIMES TO CLEAR AND BLESS A SPACE

Clearing and blessing your spaces moves negative energy out and invites good energy in. When you move into a new home or office, clear the new space *and* the one you are leaving behind (to avoid carrying the energies of the old space into the new one). Space clearing and blessing may also help when you are trying to sell your home and having difficulty, and when you buy land before you build a home. Even smaller everyday events, such as home renovations, acquiring new furniture, or decluttering your space, can be an opportunity to clear, bless, and rejuvenate your space.

These practices are also beneficial for times when you want or need a change in your life. For example, if you are traveling, you may want to clear your space to help ensure a positive experience. If you are seeking spiritual growth or are struggling in some way, clearing and blessing your space can give you a much-needed boost. You can also make this a regular routine to maintain a healthy, balanced energy around you. Try incorporating these practices around the change of seasons or during a full or new moon.

If you are facing intense events (e.g., illness, divorce, extreme stress) or if you have been in the presence of negative energy, sometimes space clearing and blessings are a necessity. If you sense any malevolent spirits or entities, use caution and find an experienced practitioner to help you.

Clearing your energy and space regularly will magickally affect all areas of your life. If some area of your life is out of balance, do a space clearing. No one is immune to accumulating unwanted energies if they are not cleansing themselves and their space regularly.

Tools for Clearing Up Energy in Space Clearing

» Rattle

» Drum (one of the best ways to break up heavy energies)

» High-quality Balinese bell (There are bells made specifically for space clearing)

» Clapping with your hands works great if you don't have a tool

» Smoke from burning white sage

» Essential oils

» Salt

» Prayer

Tools for Bringing in New Auspicious Energies and Blessing the Space

» Bells and chimes

» Your voice through song or chanting

» Essential oils

» Flower essences

» Palo santo (better for blessing the space in space clearing)

» Crystals

» Crystal singing bowl

You should also have any meaningful items related to the outcome you want in the home. For

example, if you want abundance, you might choose a pyrite crystal or some coins. If you are wanting to attract the energy of love, you might choose some rose quartz and roses. Consider having at least one item for each of the five elements. Flower essences, essential oil sprays, and holy water are wonderful ways to bring in the water element.

Remember, you need not have all the bells and whistles to perform space clearing. With minimal tools and a strong intention, you will get results. The smoke from sage with a strong intention to clear energies can be powerful, or clapping with your hands and embodying your intentions will do the job. You can get creative.

Space-Clearing Ceremony

Gather your tools and items for your altar and the ceremony.

» Altar cloth (choose a color that aligns with your intention for the clearing)

» Crystals

» Flowers

» Incense

» Essential oils

» Sea salt and small containers for it

» Sage and a feather if you are smudging

» Candles

» Fireproof container

» Offering

Clean the space and clear clutter. Put on clean, comfortable clothing: no socks or shoes so you can feel the energy through the chakras in your feet. You can keep a crystal for protection in your pocket if you wish. Because you will be stirring up energy in the home, put any food away and put animals out of the house.

Evaluate and attune to the energies of each room. Go into each room and sense the overall feeling in the room. Open a window in each room if there is one.

Find a central location for setting up your altar, ideally a large enough space to put your tools on. Build your altar, place all your sacred items and tools on it, and light a candle.

Now open up sacred space. Honor the spirits of the land you are on. Say your prayers and state your intention; you can even write it down and put it on your altar.

Ask permission to proceed with the clearing. Put your offering on the altar. You can also use incense and essential oils at the altar. NOTE: You will leave the candles and incense burning, so make sure they are in a safe place in a fireproof container.

To cleanse the space, begin in a room on the upper level of the home and work from top to bottom, throughout the house, finishing in the lower level of the home. Place salt in the corners of each room—as you break up the energy, the salt will absorb some of it and it also protects the space.

Either by clapping or with your tool, begin in one corner of the room and work either clockwise or counterclockwise. The direction is less important than that you are holding your intention, so go in the direction that feels right to you.

Work from the bottom (the floor) to the top (the ceiling). Go as high up as you can and don't worry because most energy stagnates on the ground. Focus on your breath and your intention to cleanse the space of all the heavy, stagnant energies.

You may notice your hands or tool will take on a life of its own and will guide you. Where there are

heavy energies you will feel stickiness and your drum, rattle, or clapping will sound and feel dull. Allow your sacred tools to guide you in the clearing. If you are smudging with sage, pay attention to the smoke and when it gets heavy, you will know it is clearing a lot of energy. You will also use your intuition to know how long to stay in a particular spot and when the energy has moved on.

If you are using clapping, a rattle, or a drum, you don't need to clear with sage as well. One or the other will do; however, some people want to give it an extra scrub with both and that is okay.

When you finish clearing the entire perimeter of the room and arrive at the door, clear all around the door. When you leave each room, you can seal the room by stating your intention, giving thanks, and doing anything else that feels right.

Once the entire space is cleared, go to your altar and state your prayer and blessings and close the space, always giving gratitude to all the helping spirits. Alternatively you can go back to each room and state your blessing for the space and then back to your altar to close the space. You can use a tool, your voice, or a sound instrument, such as a crystal singing bowl.

Put the clothes you wore straight into the wash. Clear your own energy by smudging with sage or taking a salt bath. If you can, leave any candles burning until they go out naturally. Leave your altar and salt out for 24 hours. After that, you can dispose of the salt by giving it back to the earth or a nearby body of water.

10
Shamanic Journey and Trance States

One of the core functions of a shaman is to journey or traverse other worlds while staying in their physical body. "To journey" means a shaman is traveling directly into other realms to receive information. This may seem supernatural to many in the modern world, but most of the universe is made up of empty space and it is within this space that the shaman wields magick. Shamans know how to traverse and communicate seamlessly among these "cosmic zones." They may use tools (such as a drum or rattle) or an induction method (such as plant medicine) to move through the multiple levels of the cosmos.

When a shaman goes on a journey, he or she may also gather information from spiritual realms to help the community or an individual for healing. For example, perhaps you are wondering what to do about a particular situation, involving someone close to you—your mind may be telling you to do one thing, to take the logical, and reasonable path, but your gut or your heart may be telling you to do another. Here is where a shamanic journey to contact your spiritual allies may help guide you.

Journeying is powerful and, when mastered effectively, it can bring about much transformation, healing, and self-revelation. It also takes practice and care. Through various rituals, tools, and practices outlined in this book, you can peek behind the curtain to uncover these spiritual forces. Be patient as you work with yourself to see which senses need to be opened and fully blossom. With time and experience, you will tap into the shaman's ability to see past physical illusion and find the inner spaces

inside ourselves—the place where we are able to see ourselves as we truly are. This is the most powerful way to heal the world.

What Is Shamanic Journeying?

A journeying shaman remains embodied while accessing another dimension of consciousness. Think of it as opening a door to the unseen world. Shamans are diving deep into the world of the subconscious. By doing so, they are going beyond the rational mind and tapping into their essence to receive spiritual advice and guidance. Because shamans have always known that we live in a connected world of tangible and intangible energy, they have learned to easily transition between these worlds.

A shaman's intention is very important as they prepare for a shamanic journey. The primary purpose is to retrieve information to help an individual or support the needs of the tribe. They must show respect to Mother Nature, the cosmos, and their spirit guides before performing their rituals; this will affect the quality of the information they receive.

A shamanic journey may appear in the mind's eye to be like inside a dream or watching a movie inside your own head. Each shaman may receive and interpret information during a journey in different ways: some may be highly visual; others may receive knowledge through a sense, a feeling, or an innate knowing; others through taste, touch, sound, or smell. The onus is on the individual shaman to understand how they best receive information through their spirit guides and helpers, so they can interpret the signs and messages along the way.

Even within the etheric, invisible world, you must learn to understand its particular language. The spiritual realms often communicate to us at our subconscious level; that is, they connect beyond everyday speech or even language. In the spirit world, they communicate mainly through symbols, metaphors, images, or an inner knowing or feeling. Our task is to build a relationship with our spirit allies and learn how to "decode" the messages.

Shamanic View of the Three Worlds Concept

Many shamanic practices and indigenous cultures all over the world teach a "three worlds" concept of the universe. The names and symbols vary, but the general principles are the same. It is a cosmic vision or framework of how shamans understand the structure of the universe and our place in it. *Cosmos* is the Greek word for both "order" and "world"—it signifies the ancient Greeks' vision that the world was harmonious and structured perfectly. This view of cosmology helps shamans explain the functions of the universe and where we came from. The most common names for the three worlds are the Lower World/Underworld, the Middle World, and the Upper World.

It is important to separate our Western view of the three worlds. For example, because of the influence of various religions such as Christianity, many people may be used to identifying the Lower World as "hell" and the Upper World as "heaven." The shamanic view of these places is quite different and serves a different function in their healing practices.

The Lower World

The Lower World or Underworld is the realm of the subconscious. When a shaman goes into this world, they are looking for emotions or traumas that have been repressed and concealed by the conscious mind. This Lower World is not a place of punishment. In many traditions, this realm is a place where the soul learns to regenerate and heal from previous lifetimes or karmic wounds. Many of our traumas and fears can be found hidden in this world—the shaman's task is to identify them and help bring the soul back into wholeness.

The Middle World

Our Middle World or Mother Earth is rich with resources and helpers—we have only to go outside and observe nature. From the stones to the water to plant allies, we have an abundance of physical and spiritual resources available right here on our planet. Your physical body also dwells in this Middle World. Learn to listen to the richness and the wisdom of your own body. It translates messages from the other worlds through this medium. That is why many shamanic practices involve embodiment—we are not working in spite of our body; we are using our body to help us directly connect with nature.

The Upper World

The Upper World is the place of the Higher Self or the higher plane of consciousness. It is who we are beyond our physical or mental self. Here we can access timeless wisdom and esoteric knowledge that has been long forgotten. This realm is also commonly where many cultural deities, gods, or goddesses reside. When we tap into this rich Upper World, we can seek our highest destiny and highest good in this lifetime.

Brain Waves and Trance States

Shamans walk between worlds, meaning they can expand their awareness by traversing from ordinary consciousness into nonordinary states of consciousness. These altered states of consciousness allow for a perception beyond the ordinary day-to-day functioning of the mind, physical body, and senses.

In this altered awareness, shamans can perceive reality without the confines of the ego, conditioning, and programming. Here they can communicate with spirits, provide healing, retrieve answers, and gain wisdom and power. This expanded state allows them the ability to tap into the collective unconscious and bring healing and higher perspectives to the community. They can see an enriched inner world, filled with signs and symbols from the universal creative force. All of their senses, both perceptible and imperceptible, are firing simultaneously.

Shamans use various induction methods (see chapters 11 and 12) to help them enter into altered states of consciousness, also known as trance states. To enter into a trance state means to move from one state of consciousness to another. You move from your physical reality to a nonordinary reality where time and space seem to disappear. A trained shaman can do this effortlessly.

Brain Waves

Science has begun to show how the brain changes during trance states. Brain waves (measured in Hertz or Hz, by cycles per second) are when neurons are communicating with one another inside the brain and simultaneously sending electrical impulses back and forth. These brain waves will vary, depending on your thoughts, actions, and emotions at any given time. They are measured by sensors placed over the scalp to detect these electrical impulses between groups of neurons inside your brain. Generally, any process, thought, or action that changes your perception or awareness has the potential to also change your brain wave.

There are five main groups of brain waves: gamma, beta, alpha, theta, and delta.

» GAMMA: Gamma waves are generally measured at 38 Hz and above. These occur during intense and highly focused activities, including extreme physical fitness (peak performance) or deep problem solving and concentration. Some researchers have even theorized that at this high frequency, our brains can tap into universal states of unconditional love, empathy, and altruism.

» BETA: Beta waves are measured between 13 and 38 Hz. This is typically during our normal waking state of alertness and focus. When in this state, our brains are engaged in problem solving, making judgments, and routine cognitive tasks.

» ALPHA: Alpha waves lie between 7 and 13 Hz. This indicates our brains are relaxed, yet still alert. Creativity flows easily in this state, and can include activities such as yoga, creative arts, music, and daydreaming. You are also

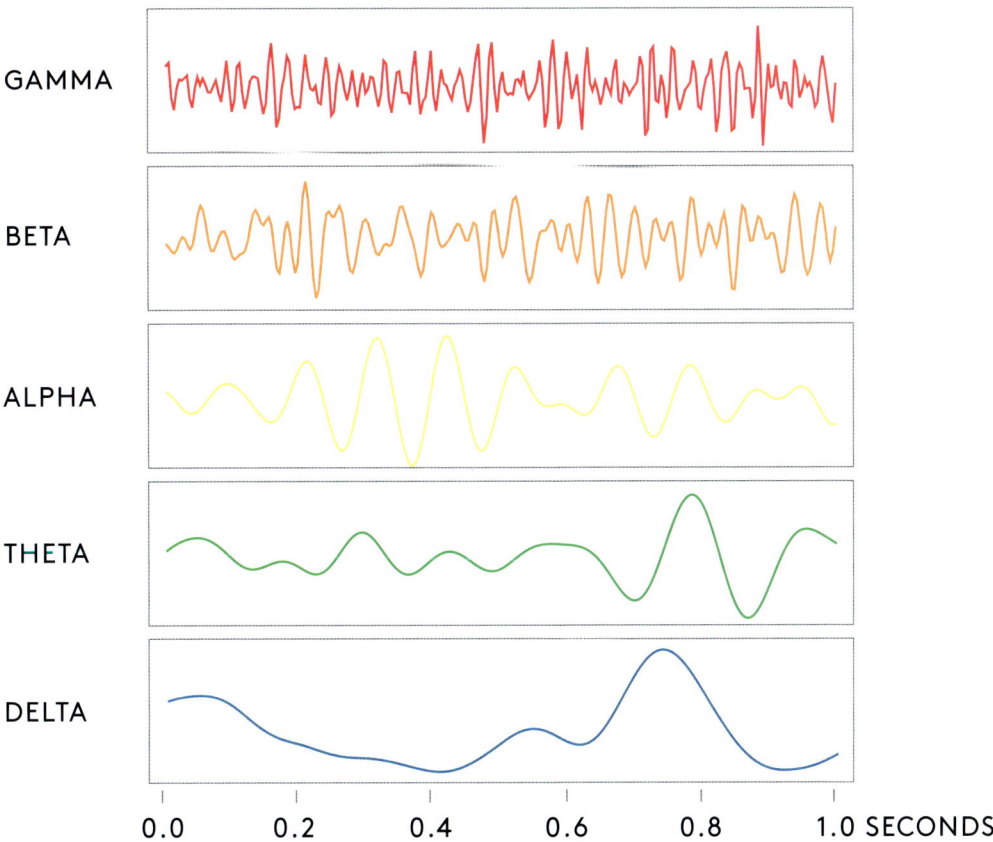

more mindful and able to live "in the now."

» THETA: Theta waves are measured between 4 and 7 Hz. Most shamans operate at this theta level state. They are in a deep state of meditation and relaxation, and they are fully tapped into their intuition. The five physical senses withdraw, and they experience conscious, waking daydreaming with clear and lucid images (also experienced as shamanic journeying). They have high memory recall, visualization, extrasensory perception, and concentration. It is also a creative state, where you are able to bask in the flow of all things.

» DELTA: Delta waves lie between 0.5 and 4 Hz. In this state, you are in a restful,

regenerative, and dreamless sleep. Your brain waves are operating at the slowest frequency. Here, your subconscious is absorbing information and allowing your body to repair itself by releasing endorphins that help relieve pain.

By being conscious and aware of which state your brain is in you can better navigate the challenges in your everyday life. From a shamanic perspective, having access to your theta wave states and beyond will enable you to access knowledge from beyond the five senses.

Altered states can be available to anyone, not only shamans. For example, you effortlessly enter in and out of altered states from the time you wake up in the morning to the time you dream at night. With practice, you can learn how to access the other worlds through shifting your consciousness intentionally.

Journeying Practice

These guidelines are highly recommended before embarking on a shamanic journey: Be in a quiet, personal space where you will not be disturbed for at least 30 minutes. Ensure you are not too hungry or thirsty and have not eaten too much (to avoid overburdening the digestive system); this can affect blood flow to the brain. Avoid alcohol or other substances for at least 24 hours prior.

Shamanic Journey

Light a candle. Open sacred space (see page 67). You may play some soft music in the background or use a rattle or drum for a slow, rhythmic beat. Always use a guide, power animal, or helping spirit.

State your intention about what you wish to learn on this journey. Sitting or lying down, pay attention to your breath and spend a few minutes relaxing the body and quieting the mind. Focus on the music or the drumbeat as you close your eyes and feel your physical senses begin to withdraw.

Bring attention to your inner mind's eye, or metaphysical third eye, as you will be journeying to receive information in the invisible world. Call on your guides or helping spirits to protect you and support you on this journey.

Begin by visualizing yourself in a place of nature. Take a moment to absorb the sights and the sounds. Where are you? In the mountains, or on a lake? Next, look for an opening, or a portal. This may be below the ground, near a cave, or at the top of the trees.

Walk through the portal with your spirit helpers beside you and allow them to show you the answers to your questions. Note any animals, angelic beings, or figures that appear—they may also have messages for you. Allow yourself to receive the information with an open heart.

Observe the way you are receiving and interpreting the information. Do you see vivid images, or do you mostly feel sensations inside your body? Do you hear voices that speak to you, or can you smell something in the distance? Let it flow to you naturally—do not force or implant messages you think you should have. Each person receives and interprets information differently; know which method works best for you. There is no right or wrong way; it's simply a matter of understanding and translating the messages in a way that is most conducive to you.

Once you have finished, return as you entered. Go through the portal once more and show gratitude to your spirit guides. Return to the same place in nature. Connect back into your body, and when you are ready, open your eyes and come back to your room and ordinary reality.

Keep a journal and write down what you have experienced.

NOTE: Shamanic journeying is a way you can discover your power animals and communicate with them. How to retrieve power animals is covered on page 164. Soul pieces can also be retrieved on a shamanic journey, this practice usually involves some training and can also be done by a trained practitioner who can journey on your behalf.

11
Shamanic Practices for Accessing Altered States of Consciousness

There are many ways to access a "trance" or ecstatic state— they are accessed during shamanic journeying and can be experienced during lucid dreaming, meditation, performing dance, music, art, hypnosis, and writing. Creativity and clarity are enhanced during an altered state, which has many health benefits, including rejuvenation, joy, stress relief, and spiritual growth.

Shamans use different tools to help them reach a nonordinary state of consciousness. Sound and music are interwoven into rituals and ceremonies, aiding in altered states, connection to spirits, emotional release, and physical healing. Dance and movement are medicines that allow you to free your mind, transcend your ego, and open the door to the spirit world. Through meditation, mantras, breathwork, and ritual, you can forge a bond with your own allies that will bring you into a new state of consciousness. Each tool serves its own special purpose, and the tools outlined here will bring you closer to a higher awareness, where you will feel connected to the universal web of creation.

Sound Is Medicine

Using sacred sound for healing has ancient origins. The first recorded culture to heal with sound was the Australian Aboriginals' use of the digeridoo. Shamans drummed, sang songs, and chanted to heal their communities. Egyptians healed by chanting with vowel sounds and the priestesses used musical instruments, such as drums rattles, tambourines, bells, cymbals, flutes, and harps. Throughout history, we see the use of sound resonance woven into our architecture in the Egyptian pyramids, Greek Asclepiad temples, churches, and cathedrals.

The phrase "music is medicine" was coined

by the Greek philosopher Pythagoras, who first discovered that sound and harmonic frequencies heal. Pythagoras taught that music can bring the faculties of the soul into harmony, compose and purify the mind, and restore health to the physical body.

Music heals via sound frequencies that travel through your body at great speed. The body is about 70 percent water and sound travels four times faster through water than it does through air. Because we are energetic beings, sound healing can break up sluggish or stagnant energy. Music is a medicine that provides stress relief, uplifts your mood, and raises your level of consciousness. Sound instruments and tools can shift you into the trance-like state of non-ordinary reality.

Sound Tools and Instruments

Music enables us to connect to the soul. Using sound frequency is the key to unlocking the doorway of healing, imagination, creativity, and expanded states of awareness. There are myriad sound tools and instruments, from the traditional drum and rattle to crystal singing bowls, gongs, chimes, bells, vocal toning, and light language. The human voice is one of the most powerful sound healing tools.

The Drum

The drum has been used by diverse cultures around the world as a sacred shamanic healing tool. Shamanic drumming is a repetitive drumbeat typically with a tempo of three to seven beats per second. This rhythm will induce trance states for shamanic journeying.

A simple rhythm to start playing the drum is the beat of one, two, three, four (repeat) beat. The heartbeat, just like the name, is the rhythm of one two, one two (repeat). Once you get more comfortable with the drum, you can learn various beats and rhythms and you will discover what feels good to you. The more you work with your drum, the more naturally it will guide you. It can even seem as though it is playing through you.

Traditional handmade animal hide-drums and nonanimal hide drums are available. You can find ceremonial courses in your local area where you can learn to make your own drum. When buying a drum, pay attention to the size, portability, color, and decorative elements. See how it plays and feels for you. Do you prefer animal hide versus vegan material? The source of the drum is important to consider as well. You may need to determine how the animal was honored while the drum was being made and confirm that the drum's maker has ethical business and sourcing practices.

The Rattle

The rhythm and sound of a shamanic rattle is one of the quickest and simplest tools you can use for shifting into an altered state. Rattles can also be used to clear heavy energies, to call in the directions and spirits, and to sing songs.

The spirit of the rattle will work with you and guide you if you ask it to. See how the rattle feels in your hand—observe the weight and the way the sounds emanate from the seeds inside of it. Notice how the seeds inside the rattle may spin or create sounds when using it around various forms of energy. Test your rattle in front of several chakra points (see page 56) on your body and see how the sound changes.

Once you have developed a trusting relationship with the spirit of your rattle, you can ask your tool for help, particularly if you're meditating. Be open to the responses you receive. Keep your heart chakra open and allow whatever messages come through the rattle to speak to your heart.

Sound Medicine Ceremony

Everything is alive, and for shamans, their sound tools are teeming with a spirit of their own. These instruments can become your allies and teachers when you connect to the essence of them. Your tools will show you how and when to use them. You will develop a relationship with them and that is when the magick and healing happens.

When you start to work with a new sound ally or instrument, it is important to honor it in ceremony. This way, you are paying respect as you get acquainted with it as a sacred tool and spirit ally.

Sound Ally Initiation

Find a quiet place by yourself. It can be in nature, in front of your altar, or anywhere that feels good to you. Set up sacred space (see page 67).

Sit with your sound tool and take long, deep breaths through the center of your heart. Call to the spirit of your sound tool. Tell it your intention to develop a relationship with it and let anything else you want to say or do happen naturally. A name for your new ally might come through.

Spend some time with it, playing it, feeling its energy, and listening to its spirit. Let it guide you. Thank your sound tool and close the space.

Dance

Movement and dance have long been used by indigenous shamans to shift consciousness and connect to the spirit world. A shamanic journey does not always involve sitting or lying down in relaxation.

Shamans often combine dance with breathwork, music, or drumming. Dance helps you step outside of the mind and allows for the release of dense, stuck energies and emotions. This creates space for you to cultivate creativity, self-actualization, and spiritual growth; you experience a deeper connection to your heart and develop a sense of embodiment.

Ecstatic dance is a form of dance practiced throughout history by different cultures. In shamanic traditions, ecstatic dance was used alongside drumming to induce altered states of consciousness.

Modern-day dance practices that are rooted in shamanism include 5Rhythmes, ecstatic and trance dance. There are countless intentional dance and movement practices that quiet the mind and shift consciousness, such as yoga, tai chi, martial arts, and qigong.

Dance Ceremony

Find a space large enough for you to freely dance and move around. Turn on some music. It is helpful to have a playlist of songs you enjoy already prepared.

Drop your awareness from your brain into your heart (see the Quick Coherence Technique on page 60).

Begin to slowly move your body in ways and patterns that make you feel connected and in tune with the music. Continue to keep your attention in your body and on your breath.

Let your body move in any way that is desires. This is not meant to be choreographed or structured movements. Let the movements become intuitive without labeling them or putting any judgments on them. Allow whatever experiences you need to come forth. Your body will know what it's asking for.

Continue to stay embodied and dance until you are ready to stop.

Meditation

Meditation techniques have been practiced by spiritual groups and cultures around the globe. Eastern traditions such as Buddhism, Hinduism, and Taoism have been the most widely studied by scientific research. The brain imaging of meditators has been shown to induce altered states of consciousness.

Meditation techniques can vary from focusing on your breathing to something specific, such as an object (e.g., a candle) or a word or phrase (e.g., a mantra). The goal is not to identify with the thinking mind, but to let the thoughts pass by without attaching to them. This allows you to be an observer of your internal state.

Research has shown that meditation can reduce stress and depression and promote relaxation and overall well-being. Scientific studies have proven that regular meditation can have profound effects on the brain, such as increased alpha and theta waves (see page 130). Long-term meditation has been shown to open up access to a larger area of the brain and synchronize the left and right hemispheres to a greater degree. It was discovered that long-term daily meditation by Tibetan Buddhist monks showed that several areas of their brain were permanently altered, allowing them to ascend to higher spiritual states.

A regular meditation practice can help bring awareness into the present moment. Simply keep an awareness on your breath or notice the sensations of breathing. Your awareness cannot focus on two things simultaneously. When you shift your awareness from your stream of thinking and into your body, focusing on your breathing allows you to silence the mind. When the mind chatter begins again, simply observe it, and bring your attention back into your body and breath.

Hundreds of forms of meditation exist. Some of the more commonly known practices are yoga, Zen, mindfulness meditation, silent meditation retreats, Transcendental Meditation, mantra meditation, and breathwork meditation.

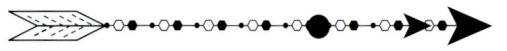

BOX BREATHING

Focus on your breath as a way to find inner calm, tune into your energy, and prepare for meditation. Find a comfortable place, sitting or lying down, with your eyes closed. Breathe in through your nose while slowly counting to four. Hold your breath while counting slowly to four. Stay relaxed while you avoid inhaling or exhaling for a count of four. Begin to slowly exhale for a count of four.

Do several rounds of this for at least 4 minutes, or until calm returns. If four counts is challenging to start with, you can count to three instead of four. Once you are used to the technique, you can count from five up to seven.

Mantras

A mantra is a group of words or syllables, and chanting mantras is an ancient form of meditation practice. Mantras all carry a unique energetic frequency imprint from thousands of years of being chanted. We belong to an interconnected energy field matrix and when you recite a mantra, you tap into the energetic field of that mantra. This means the power from the mantra is amplified from the collective energetic field created by all those who have chanted it across countless lifetimes.

Chanting and repeating a mantra creates a sound

vibration that generates an energy circuit throughout the body. This sound vibration from the chanting distracts the brain, quiets the mind, brings relaxation, and can facilitate entering into trance states. In addition to shifting your consciousness, chanting has other benefits. The sound creates a vibration that relaxes the nervous system, boosts the immune system, releases endorphins, and reduces stress. The sound vibrations break up stuck energies in the energetic body, and clear and activate the chakras.

Chanting can include sacred words, mantras, and prayers and are recited in many different languages. Some mantras have literal meanings and others do not. The earliest mantras date to India more than three thousand years ago and were written in Vedic Sanskrit.

Mantras can be chanted out loud, sung, whispered, or recited silently. Another common practice is the use of mala or prayer beads held inside the hands while chanting mantras. The benefits of mantras can be achieved by repeating anything with focused attention. By doing so, you are creating neural pathways in your brain to aid in relaxation, focus, and positive thinking.

You can chant with the mantra Aum, one of the most widely used mantras from the Hindu tradition. Aum is a sacred sound that signifies the entirety of the universe. Another suggestion is the ancient Buddhist mantra *Om Mani Padmi Om*, a Sanskrit word pronounced "OHM-MAH-NEE-PAHD-MAY-HUM." The translation is "praise to the jewel in the lotus."

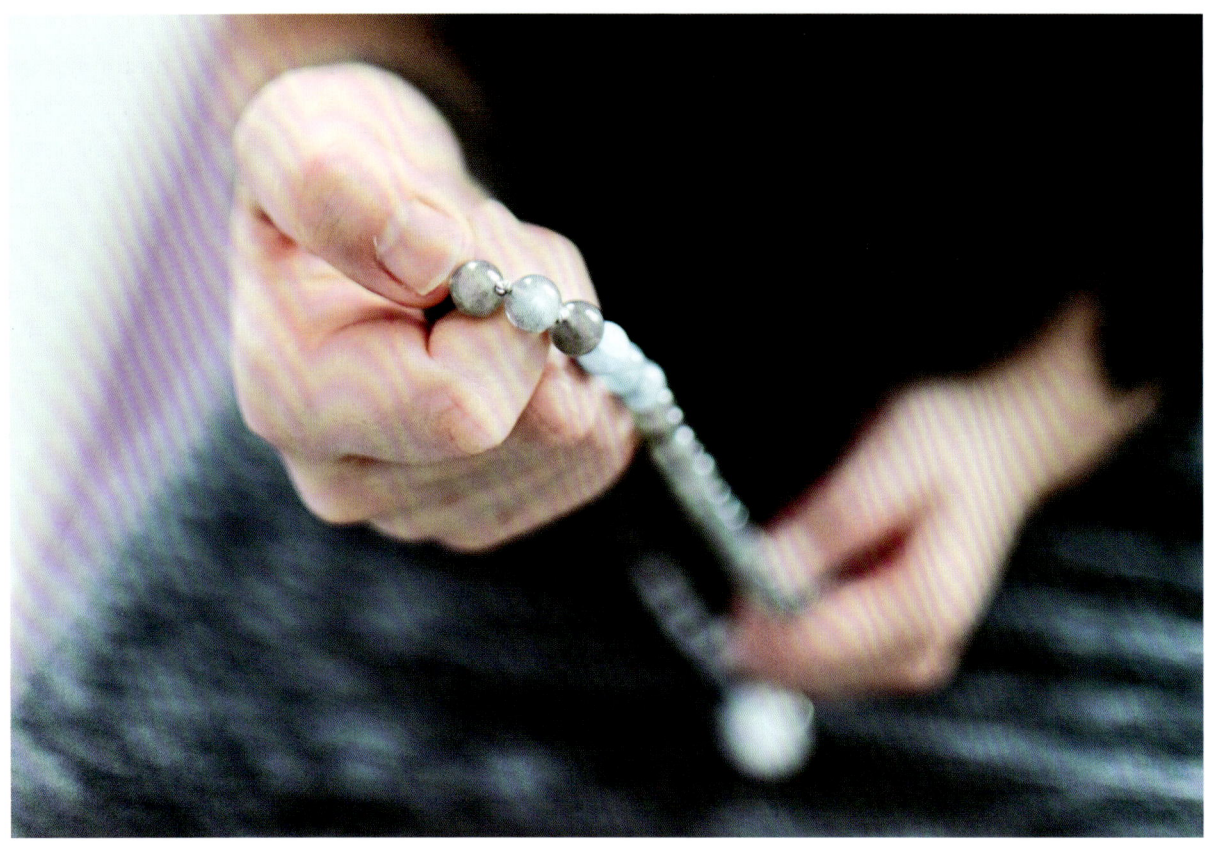

When you chant *Om Mani Padmi Hum*, contemplate the meaning of each word in the mantra:

» OM—divine energy, generosity, dissolves the ego; the sound of the universe

» Ma—purifies jealousy and the practice of ethics

» Ni—tolerance and patience

» Pad—perseverance, release of judgment

» Me—concentration, release of attachments

» Hum—wisdom and unity

Mantra Meditation

Lie or sit in a comfortable position, with your mala beads (if you use them). Choose a word, phrase, or mantra to focus on. Close your eyes and slow your breathing down, taking long inhales, and exhales. Harmonize your heart and brain by doing the Quick Coherence Technique (see page 60).

Recite the mantra silently or out loud with the natural rhythm of your breath. The mantra can be split half on the inhale and the other half on the exhale, or you can repeat it on both. You will find a rhythm that feels right.

Experiment with repeating the mantra out loud and internally and notice how the vibrations feel in your body. When thoughts arise, simply bring your attention back to the mantra.

Continue for 5 to 30 minutes or however long you wish. When you are finished, take deep breaths and notice how you feel.

Breathwork

Expanding awareness through the use of breathwork has been used for centuries by shamanic cultures. It is one of the simplest and most accessible ways to enter into nonordinary reality. In this state, the mind becomes silent and ego steps aside. Experiences can range from relaxation to bliss states to communication with divine beings or the Higher Self. Connecting to the breath helps the release of old patterns and traumas, including memories of past lives. Often lower emotions of fear, grief, anger, and sadness can also to be transmuted.

The idea that breath is Spirit has long been considered by many traditions around the world. This means that breath is the physical air that enters into the lungs, but it is also the spiritual source (energy) that creates life. For example, in Hindu philosophy, the Sanskrit word *prana* means "breath" and is also seen as the universal energy or "vital life force." "Spirit" or "soul" is the translation for the word *breath*, derived from the Latin word *spiritus*.

Breathwork has roots in Western psychotherapy and in Eastern practices such as Buddhism, yoga, and tai chi. Today, there are a multitude of unique forms of breathwork because it is simple, effective, and accessible. Modern breathwork can bring in elements such as talk therapy, bodywork, art, music, dance, and various breathing techniques. Holotropic Breathwork and rebirthing are some of the older forms of breathwork that were born in the 1960s. Newer types of breathwork techniques continue to emerge, including Transcendental Breathwork and the Wim Hof Method.

During a breathwork session, the body is flooded with increased oxygen and with vital energy. The synergy between the breath and energy breaks up stagnant emotions and heavy energies. Breathwork can be practiced in the comfort of your home or facilitated by a practitioner in a private session or group setting.

Breathwork Ceremony

Circular breathing is a way to reduce stress, clear your mind, and return your breath to its natural rhythm.

Find a comfortable space to lie down; have an eye mask and an extra blanket in case you get cold. Set up sacred space (see page 67). It is suggested to have a partner who can hold space for you. Start with 20 minutes (for the first time) and then switch with your partner.

Close your eyes and relax. Take slow, deep breaths in and out through your mouth. Breathe into the belly, and when you are almost full, immediately exhale. When you feel almost empty, inhale again. And repeat. Speed your breathing up a little faster than normal without straining to breathe, and allow it to be natural and relaxed. Imagine the breath like a wave, coming in, and going out. There are no pauses between the breaths, just continuous breathing.

Your body will eventually find its own rhythm, connect to the breath, and become immersed in it. Let it take you where it wants to go. Around 15 minutes in you will enter into an altered state. It is normal for you to feel tingling sensations in your face, body, and extremities; emotional release, states of bliss, and euphoria can also occur.

After 20 minutes your partner will gently call you back by asking you to slowly return. Take some time and notice how you feel. When you feel ready, journal or draw anything important you want to remember. Sometimes when you return fully, you may have forgotten part of the experience.

12
Sacred Plant Medicines

Mother Earth has blessed us with an enormous plant kingdom, providing us with our most natural ways to heal. Since the beginning of time, the ancients aligned with the spirits of the plants as allies. These plant spirits were integral to their day-to-day life, as part of their healing, empowerment, and guidance. They knew that the plant spirits were there to teach them.

They worked with all types of plants for cooking and to cure illness and disease. Some also used what are commonly called psychedelic, hallucinogenic, and entheogenic plants as sacred medicines. These visionary plants allowed them to access altered states of consciousness and enter into the spirit world for the purposes of healing. Sacred plant medicines were central to our ancestors' health and well-being. They revered plant medicines as natural gifts given to us from Mother Earth. Plant use was woven into their culture and traditions, spiritual practices, ceremonies, and healing rituals.

Today, some feel the call to these sacred plant medicines because they are ready for a shift in consciousness, to release their patterns and heal their lineage. Our connection to nature and to the plant kingdom has been lost for so many of us. Sacred plant medicines teach us our innate connection to the higher vibrational plane of nature. They show us

how to become still within and more present, flexible, and resilient. They offer a way to healing and to discovering our divinity, and in that sacred space we can rapidly shed things that no longer serve us. Plant medicines—when used properly and appropriately, in a ceremonial way with reverence for the spirits of the plants—may bring about profound healing.

Not all plant medicines are for everyone, and not all shamans choose the path of using psychedelics for entering into altered states of consciousness for healing. Everyone is on their own unique journey and has their own individual soul purpose. For those who are called to use plant medicines, this section explains them in the context of shamanism: why and how to respect the plants; how to use them with gratitude, humility, compassion, and openness; and how to treat them as sacred.

Questions to Ask Before Using Sacred Medicine

This short introduction to some sacred plant medicines explains some of their potential benefits and ways to use them. It also includes important points to be aware of about each specific medicine. Before you decide to use plant medicines, be sure to ask yourself the following questions:

» Have I researched this plant medicine extensively to learn its benefits and potential side effects?

» Have I consulted a trained practitioner on responsible use of this medicine?

» Have I consulted the shaman or facilitator, and do I trust them?

» Do I have an intention for using this medicine?

» Am I prepared to integrate what I learn?

» Am I aware of any legal constraints regarding possession or use of this medicine?

Plant Medicine Preparation

Set up a safe, sacred space that is appropriate for your needs (e.g., a group, individual use, or as a component of dance or art). Bring any crystals that you want to use for journeying or protection.

Set your intention. You can ask yourself questions: Why am I sitting in ceremony? What aspect of myself do I wish to explore? In what area of my life do I wish to receive clarity? Where do I want to bring in more love, ease, and joy?

Call in your Higher Self, spirit allies, spirit animals, and helpers. Always call in the spirit of the plant that you are working with. Protection is needed when entering into other realms through plant medicines; ask for protection, envision your entire auric field in a protective bubble, and affirm you and your space is clear and protected. Ask for what you want from the plants, as they respond to your asking. State your intention for the ceremony, for example, "Great Spirit, sacred ones, I call to you to be here with me. I call my helping spirits, guides, guardians and beings of light into my space. I call in the spirit of Grandmother Cacao; as my plant medicine teacher, teach me what I need, and show me, guide me, and protect me. I ask for healing and release of all my fear around stepping into my power. I ask that this healing is for my highest good. I give thanks for this medicine and the spirits of this land. Thank you, and, so it is, Aho."

Plant Medicines

This introduction to some commonly used plant medicines will give you some of the benefits, ways in which to use them, and some important points to be aware of with regard to each specific medicine.

This chapter is also a very short introduction into the complexity and diversity of some of the more commonly used plant medicines among shamans. It is recognized that while some of them are still illegal in many countries, their use for healing and ceremony has prevailed among shamans, religious practitioners, and spiritual groups. While their use is certainly not for everyone, it is necessary to touch on these sacred medicines for those embarking on the shamanic path who want to learn more about them and their benefits. Those who feel the call to connect deeply with Mother Nature may do so through sacred plants.

Cacao

Sacred cacao is a gentle, yet powerful, plant medicine. It was used by the Olmec, Aztecs, and Mayans in their spiritual rituals, celebrations, and ceremonies, and they considered the plant a gift from the gods. Cacao is the primary ingredient in chocolate, but chocolate has a lower content of actual cacao and has been altered by adding sugar, milk, and other ingredients. Ceremonial cacao is 100 percent cacao cultivated and harvested for ceremonial purposes. It is the highest grade cacao; nothing has been added or taken away from the cacao seed.

Cacao contains theobromine, which differs from caffeine yet acts in a similar fashion: caffeine affects the central nervous system and theobromine affects the cardiovascular system (heart). Physiologically, theobromine stimulates blood flow to the heart and the brain and expands the vascular system around the heart by as much as 40 percent.

Cacao expands the energy field of the heart and opens up the heart chakra, assisting emotional releases and transcendence to joy, love, and bliss states. In shamanism, sacred cacao is a divine feminine plant spirit teacher: she invites you to embrace your sensuality and sexuality. The cacao spirit is a keeper of ancient wisdom, a loving intelligence that will teach you or show you what you need.

As a medicine, cacao reduces mind chatter, allowing for the flow of direct knowledge and wisdom from your Higher Self and spirit helpers. It brings a deeper connection and grounding to the Earth. It also increases alertness, concentration, and focus, making it a great ally for meditation, writing, and any creative outlets. With an open heart, you have increased intuition, gratitude, and connection to others. Cacao combined with various forms of dance and movement can guide you deeper into the feminine.

If you choose to use cacao, be sure to get it from a reliable, trusted source. Be aware that it is a cardiac stimulant and can cause side effects such as headache and stomach cramps. Do your research and be responsible, and always be sure to consult a health-care provider if needed to discuss your specific situation.

Cacao Ceremony: Heart-Opening Medicine

Cacao can enhance a connection to the spirit world and altered states. Each experience will be different because you are always different. It also can be a part of group or individual ceremonies, along with meditation, dance, and celebration.

To make ceremonial cacao, you will need:

2 ounces ceremonial-grade cacao

1 cup (235 ml) boiling water

Optional: nut or oat milk; 1 teaspoon of maple syrup; a pinch of cayenne pepper, cinnamon, or cardamom

In a mug, whisk or blend the cacao and water until frothy. Add any optional ingredients.

When your ceremonial cacao is ready, open up sacred space. Call in the spirit of cacao, sit with your cacao in prayer, and set your intentions.

Mindfully sip your delicious drink while remaining open in your heart chakra and allow whatever wants to come. Ask questions and sit with a journal and write what comes. Always give thanks for the wisdom and insights received.

Cannabis

Cannabis, also known as marijuana, was widely used for its healing and medicinal benefits by many ancient cultures from Asia to Europe. There is also evidence that marijuana was used as a sacrament for religious, shamanic, and spiritual purposes. Cannabis seeds were found in the graves of the shamans in Siberia and China from as early as 500 BCE. At various times, cannabis has been deemed an illegal substance. The laws around marijuana are evolving and its use is becoming legal in most of North America. Today, in many places it is legal to use medical marijuana for ailments such as chronic pain, HIV, and cancer.

Tetrahydrocannabinol (THC) is the chemical component in cannabis that causes the psychoactive aspects that allow for altered states of consciousness. When using cannabis for ceremony and journeying, it is important to open up sacred space and have an intention. Cannabis ceremonies are sacred. When used with intention, cannabis amplifies, energizes, and opens up the psyche, and you can access answers and inner guidance. When used for spiritual purposes, deep and profound experiences can occur.

If you choose to explore this plant, use caution, follow local laws, and consult a health practitioner when needed. You will also want to pay careful attention to which strains and dosages are the best for you. There are many different strains and potencies of cannabis and ways to consume it—from smoking to edibles. Some strains are more uplifting and creative (stavia); others are more relaxing and sedative (indica). Develop a relationship with cannabis and learn how it works specifically for you. Also keep in mind that cannabis has often been used as more of a recreational drug that does not honor the spirit of the cannabis plant. As with all plant medicines, when they are abused, they don't serve the higher purpose and vibrations of the plant.

Psilocybin (Mushrooms)

Mushrooms are a fungi that contain the psychoactive compound psilocybin, a naturally occurring psychedelic compound. There are more than 180 species of mushrooms all over the world.

Commonly known as "magic mushrooms" or "shrooms," psilocybin mushrooms have been studied in therapeutic and psychiatric settings and have shown to treat addiction, anxiety, depression, post-traumatic stress disorder, obsessive-compulsive disorder, and other mental health disorders. Mushrooms can be eaten in their dried whole or powdered form. Mushroom tea and mushroom chocolates make them taste better and help mask their strong flavor.

Mushrooms have a rich history of being revered as sacred medicines by spiritual and shamanic cultures, and they were used to enter into altered states of consciousness to communicate with spirits for healing. On the shamanic path, these substances are always used with respect and within a ceremony. This sacred plant medicine can expand consciousness, enhance creativity, and increase self-awareness. It may also release and heal stuck traumas, emotional blocks, negative thought forms, heavy energies, and limited thinking.

If you choose to explore psilocybin mushrooms as part of your shamanic path, be aware that mushrooms are illegal at the federal level and are categorized as a Schedule I controlled substance in the United States. They are decriminalized in some North American cities and are legal in some controlled settings in human studies for their potential psychiatric and medical benefits.

Ayahuasca

Ayahuasca is a visionary medicine that is revered in shamanic healing ceremonies. It is a brew of at least two plants: the vine (*Banisteriopsis caapi*) and most often the leaf (*Psychotria viridis* or *Diplopterys cabrerana*). The combination of the two plants produces its healing and visionary effects. Ayahuasca is a feminine plant medicine, considered to be the "mother of all plants," and one of her purposes is to teach us about the plant kingdom and how to communicate with them as spirit allies.

Ayahuasca ceremonies are used for physical, emotional, mental, and spiritual healing. Often dietary adjustments, referred to as a dieta or fast, are required before the ceremony to purify and prepare the body. The experience can be unpredictable because ayahuasca can show you what you need to see or what you need to feel in order to heal your traumas and energetic imbalances. For some people, it can offer enhanced creativity, joy, and deeper connection to others. For others, it may help release fears and trauma. Ayahuasca teaches you love and unity. There is no ego, there is no separation. She shows you the truth of who you really are.

If you feel called to explore ayahuasca (whether locally or abroad), proceed with caution in researching and finding a reputable shaman. Interview them beforehand to ask questions and develop trust. If you are traveling to South America, it is best to travel with someone else and research the retreat center you are going to. Do your due diligence, as you want to be in a safe and protected setting when you are working with ayahuasca.

San Pedro Cactus

San Pedro cactus (*Echinopsis pachanoi*) is a plant native to the South Americas in the Andean mountains of Ecuador and Peru and has been used for several thousand years. It is similar to peyote, both of which contain the psychoactive alkaloid known as mescaline.

San Pedro cactus is a male plant spirit and a heart-chakra opener. It will bring you into your right, creative brain while the left, thinking brain steps aside, making it difficult to use technology or tasks that require a lot of movement and thinking. Everything slows down with this sacred plant medicine. It allows you to reside in the present moment, opening you up to bliss states. San Pedro can be visual, and it can also be very emotional: releases such as laughter, crying, or vomiting can occur. A San Pedro journey usually lasts about 10 to 12 hours and can be a beautiful, sacred plant medicine to do with your partner, as it can facilitate connection.

San Pedro can be taken in a powder form as a drink or in a capsule or freshly made from the cactus. Source and preparation are important. San Pedro can be hard on the stomach for some people. It is helpful to fast the night before or have an empty stomach to prevent the onset of nausea, which can occur. Set up everything you might need, including water and a bucket. Ensure the environment is safe and private; being out in nature is ideal. For your first time, it is beneficial to have a facilitator.

13
Healing Tools
of the Shaman

Shamanic practices involve knowing that everything is connected through a universal energy web of life and to the unseen world. Everything is sacred and everything has spirit. This multidimensional world we live in is here to assist us when we realize our true nature. Shamans are the seers and knowers. They are the bridge between the other world and us—bringing back knowledge and wisdom for our evolution and healing of body, emotions, mind, and spirit.

Shamans see everything as sacred, and because of that they respect and honor the spirit in all things. They have reverence and pay homage to the spirits, guides, and ancestors they work with. They honor the spaces they are in, the land they work on, the Four Directions, the animals, Father Sky, and Mother Earth. They have sacred ways in how they pay their respect and show gratitude. The shamanic world opens you up to your deep connection to all things, to nature, and to Mother Earth and as a result you see all of life as a sacred offering.

Shamans have various treasures and sacred tools that assist them in their practices. Many of the ways of the shaman have been used since the beginning of time and have been passed down orally or in sacred texts. There are civilizations we may never read about in a book, but the memory and wisdom of them is stored within our spirit and DNA. Our helping ancestors and spirits of the unseen world generously share their knowledge with us again and again.

Sacred Offerings

Making offerings to ancestors, guides, guardians, angels, helping spirits, and gods and goddesses is an ancient traditional practice and customary way

to acknowledge and honor the spirits in the other world, a way to give gratitude to the Creator, to God, to the Universal Source. The offering is a way to say thank you to the spirits. When appreciated, the spirits are energized, and in return are happy and motivated to assist.

Offerings are also a form of energy exchange. Life is an eternal dance of what shamans call *ayni*, which is about giving and receiving energy. An offering says thank you. It shows them you are aware of their presence and your connection to them. Giving an offering at a sacred site and on pilgrimages shows the spirits of the land, the ones who walked here before you, that you offer reciprocity and gratitude.

Offerings to the spirts can be made before a ceremony—they are often put on altars. If the ceremony is outdoors or at a sacred site, offerings can be made to the spirits of the land. They can also be left on an altar in the home. The spirits of the unseen world love offerings.

How to Choose an Offering

Put care and thought into what you offer the spirits. Choose an offering that comes from the heart—some traditions call them heart gifts. Consider where the offering comes from—the energy behind where and how things are harvested, produced, and handled is important.

The good thing is there are so many options when it comes to offerings. It is very common to offer food—spirits just happen to love sweets. Cakes, desserts, honey, chocolate, and dried fruit are good options. Herbs, plants, seeds, nuts, tobacco, wine, fruit, stones, crystals, fabrics, sage, and flowers are also common offerings. You can even gather acorns, wood bark, and pine cones. Even an offering of song and dance is acceptable.

Offerings are also brought by participants to ceremonies for the spirits and often the shamans will be gifted anything from stones to sage, herbs, plants, or food for energy exchange from all the effort put into the ceremony.

When you bring offerings into your prayers, ceremonies, and life, you are in a state of giving and in gratitude. It is a universal law that what you can give comes back to you. You will see the power of giving offerings through the magick in your ceremonies and the results when your intentions are manifested.

Despacho

A despacho is a sacred offering commonly made in Peru and elsewhere in South America. It is a nature mandala filled with beautiful objects that represent our gratitude and love for Mother Nature. It is also an outward exchange of reciprocity between us and the Earth. Despachos can be made for many reasons: to honor the nature spirits, to ask for abundance and blessings, to make special requests such as guidance for your love life or career, or even to make atonement.

Before creating a despacho, always be aware of your intention. Why are you making the despacho and what is the intended purpose and outcome? While you are making it, ensure you have opened sacred space first, and select and place each item with the utmost care and respect. Here is one way to make a despacho:

» A white rectangular piece of paper you can fold up easily

» A half shell (clam or scallop) or circular object to represent the divine feminine

» Two sticks that make a cross to represent the divine masculine

- » 12 or more well-formed bay leaves
- » White flowers to represent the divine masculine
- » Red flowers to represent the divine feminine
- » Sugar to represent sweetness for Mother Earth
- » Rice for abundance and fertility
- » Sweets that you can crumble, such as cookies or crackers

Other offerings you may include: herbs, incense, chocolate, beans, kernels of corn, stones, and crystals

- » Paper money
- » Red wine
- » Colorful string

Place the white piece of paper flat on the ground. Put the shell open side up in the center. Position the two sticks inside the shell.

Prepare the k'intu bundles: Place three bay leaves with the veiny side facing down. Add one white petal and one red petal from the flowers. Repeat to make four bundles for the Four Directions, up to twelve bundles total. Blow gently into each bundle with your prayers and requests. Place each bundle clockwise around the shell and sticks.

While placing each item into your despacho, ensure you are infusing each object with your finest energies and highest intentions. Add the other ingredients: Sprinkle the sugar in a clockwise motion around the k'intu bundles. Do the same for the rice. Add the cookies, beans, herbs, and paper money.

Splash a few drops of red wine into the despacho. Wrap a colorful string around the entire offering in a circle.

Once complete, fold the white paper to close it. Tie it like a parcel with either white or red string. You can choose to either burn or bury your despacho. Allow the energies you have created to release into the cosmos and detach yourself from the outcome.

Power Objects and Sacred Tools

Shamans make use of power objects that are meaningful sacred tools and symbols—they serve as allies in the work they do. A power object is used with intention and to serve a specific purpose. An object does not inherently have power—it is the shaman's reverence and connection to the object that gives it its powers. Power is a gift from spirit. A power object allows spiritual life force energy to become tangible in a physical form. Just as shamans are a channel for energy, power objects are also channels for energy. Through the shaman's intent, the object acts as a conduit for spirit. Power objects are alive and have spirit embodied within them.

A shaman may utilize certain sacred objects depending on the culture they belong to. Shamans may use no tools at all or only a few tools in their practice. They might be called to an object through intuition, visions, or guidance from the spirits during journeys. Objects might come to them in an unexpected way or arrive as gifts. It is common for sacred objects to find you. It is also important to know that not all sacred objects have an actual presence in the physical earth. During journeys, a shaman will ask their spirit helpers or power animals for metaphorical tools that will imbue them with power for protection, healing, and divination.

What Are Power Objects Used For?

Power objects can be used for shamanic journeying, moving stagnant energies from the human energy field and from homes and workspaces. They can be used in ceremonies to call in the spirits, for blessings and prayers. They can be used for song, dance, meditation, and dreamwork. You can place your power objects on your altar to charge and amplify their energies. A power object has symbolic meanings and serves as a bridge between you and your Higher Self, nature, and the spirit world.

During ceremony, the sacred tool is a form of communication and can show the shaman nonverbal information from spirit. For example, when using a drum over a person during a healing ceremony, the drumbeat will sound and feel different over areas of stagnant unwanted energies.

How Do You Choose a Power Object?

In shamanism, everything is alive, everything is connected, and everything is sacred; thus, the options for power objects can be endless. Choosing a power object can be very personal and similar to choosing a new crystal or piece of clothing: you choose what you are attracted to and often the object will choose you. If you want a power object for a particular purpose, you can set your intention to find one and see what shows up for you.

A power object can be handcrafted (e.g., a drum or a rattle). When you create something yourself, you develop a connection to it by infusing it with your intentions, prayers, and gratitude. This process activates and amplifies the energies of your objects, giving them power. A sacred power object can be something from nature or can be manufactured. Whether the power object is handmade, gifted, found, or purchased, it is your personal relationship with the object that imbues it with power.

Traditional and Common Power Objects

SOUND TOOLS: These include drums, rattles, chimes, tingsha, crystal singing bowls, harps, gongs, and various other instruments. Remember that sound tools are often very personal because of the connection developed. Out of respect, don't play anyone's sound tool without permission. For more on using sound tools, see page 137.

MEDICINE OR TALKING STICKS: This is a traditional power object used for speaking prayers and can be used during ceremony. Whomever is holding the stick is the only person speaking. They hold the power in their voice to speak their truth and everyone else holds space and respectfully listens. This way, the person with the stick is not interrupted. In circles, the stick will be passed around to everyone and each person will have a turn with it. Talking sticks teach you how to honor the sacred wisdom of the trees, by holding space, listening, and being flexible.

FEATHERS: Bird feathers represent the air element (see page 82). They connect spirit, the bird, and the person using it. Feathers are used to cleanse items, living spaces, and human energy fields. They are also commonly used in shamanic ceremonies, rituals, and journeys. Feathers are used as sacred tools to remove heavy, stagnant, and unwanted energies. They can be swept through a person's auric field to cleanse it and are very effective for clearing away heavy emotions. Feathers can be used along with the sacred herbs of sage, palo santo, and sweetgrass for smudging, energizing, and blessing. They are also used to give blessings and during celebrations. Symbolic of freedom and connection to the spirit world, feathers allow you to send questions and prayers to the Upper World on their wings. Seeing a feather on the ground as you walk or having a feather appear is thought of as a sign or message by a deceased loved one or an angel. Some feathers are illegal to possess (even if it was found), so research any feathers you might find or want to purchase, just to be certain.

THE MEANINGS OF FEATHERS

Different feathers evoke different powers and energies depending on the bird. Some of the common feathers and their symbolic meaning are:

CROW: protection, destiny, fearlessness, ancient wisdom, trickster energy

EAGLE: reaching your higher purpose, the spirit world, strength, power

HAWK: strength, messages from spirit, farsightedness, guardianship, clarity

OWL: magick, intuition, seeing in the dark (seeing what is hidden), wisdom

TURKEY: fertility, abundance, fullness of life, pride, generosity

WALKING STICK: Also known as a staff or medicine stick, a walking stick was historically used in many civilizations and shamanic cultures around the world. The staff was revered as a symbol of leadership and authority. The walking stick had several other uses, including as a weapon, for assistance when traveling long distances, and when carved on, to keep records and tell stories. A shaman's staff also connects them to the realms of the Upper, Middle, and Lower Worlds (chapter 10) and is used as a sacred tool for ceremony. A staff is commonly made from wood and often adorned with symbols, carvings, talismans, stones, feathers, beads, and leather. You can purchase a staff already made or you can get creative and make one yourself.

CRYSTALS AND STONES: These serve many functions and are powerful healing allies. Crystals come in rough and raw forms, polished, or carved objects (such as knives for cutting cords). The varieties and options are endless. Crystals are covered in great detail in chapter 7.

FIGURINES: Gurus, gods, goddesses, angels, animals, and symbols are often placed on altars for worship and prayer. They can bring in the energies of that deity—for instance, the goddess Kuan Yin for kindness and compassion.

DIVINATION TOOLS: These include tarot cards, runes, and pendulums for receiving guidance and for doing healing work. These can be made from crystals, stones, or metals, and they can also come in the form of bracelets, necklaces, amulets, and jewelry. These items can be purchased or handmade. Infuse them with your intensions and cleanse them regularly.

REPRESENTATIONS OF THE ELEMENTS: For example us a shell for water, a lit candle for fire, a stick for earth, a feather for air, and something white for Akasha. For more about the elements, see chapter 6.

KNIVES AND SWORDS: These are used for various ritual and ceremonial purposes, such as for cutting energetic cords, for protection, and to extract energies.

SACRED PIPE: The legend of the Lakota and other tribes tells of a holy figure, the White Buffalo Calf Woman, who came to the people, taught them ceremonies, delivered the sacred pipe, also known as a *chanupa*, and taught them how to pray to the Great Spirit with it.

DREAM CATCHER: Traditionally used in Native American cultures, the dream catcher originated with the Ojibwe and Lakota nations. They are used as talismans for protection to capture any bad dreams and to allow good dreams to flow in.

MESA: A shaman's mesa, or medicine bundle, is a portable altar originating from Peru. The mesa is used in several shamanic lineages and has varying cultural and individual uses, serving as an entryway into the unseen world. It is used for ceremony, healing, prayer, connection to the spirit world, and divination. The mesa is a cloth or bag and typically contains various sacred items, such as crystals, stones, and other power objects. A mesa is a very personal sacred tool, representing your own healing journey and spiritual work.

INVISIBLE OBJECTS: An invisible cloak is a great way to protect yourself from lower level energies and entities. Envision a cloak of protection around you, sealing you from any unwanted outside influences and affirming that you are protected. The cloak can be used during any journey, group work, or when you want to shield yourself. You may also want to use a specific color such as gold light or platinum silver.

Ceremony for Power Objects

When you work with a new power object, you want to build a relationship with it. To connect with your sacred object, you will be using the five elements to bless and call in power to your object.

» Brown or green altar cloth or material

» White sage

» Lighter

» Candle

» Object(s) you wish to bless

» Clean water

» Cup or chalice

» Sound instrument (can be your voice)

» Cedar or any woody essential oil

» An offering, suggestions: 3 roses or other flowers

» Shell or glass bowl

Find a quiet place, preferably in nature near some clean running water. Bring all of your supplies. Set up your items on the altar cloth.

Cleanse yourself, the space around you, and your objects with sage (see page 113). Open up sacred space (see page 67). Put your offering on the altar and give thanks. State your intention to clear, bless, and energize your sacred tools.

Fire element: Light the candle and carefully pass your object through the flame. Ask the spirit of fire to clear and purify your object.

Water element: If you are outdoors near water, run some water over your object or use the water in your chalice. If it is an object that can't get wet, use your hands to bring the energies of the water into your object. Ask the spirit of the water to cleanse and bless your sacred tool with intuition and flow.

Air element: Hold your object up in the air,

allowing the wind to pass through it. Ask the spirits of the wind to bless your object with flexibility.

Earth element: Place your object on the earth or the altar cloth. Ask Mother Earth and the earth spirits to bless your sacred object with strength and protection.

Akasha: Using a sound instrument, infuse your object with high vibrational sounds and energy. If you are using your voice, you can sing anything that comes up or you can chant the mantra Aum (see page 141).

Put a few drops of essential oil in your hands and rub them together, cup your hands around your face, and inhale the smell while connecting to the spirit of the essential oil. Hold your hands over your altar cloth and your sacred items, bless them, and state your intention and purpose for using the items; speak any other words that arise.

Thank the elements and any other helping spirits and close the space.

Once you have blessed your sacred tools, you must continue to honor and maintain them. Power objects need to be energetically cleared and charged because as you use them, they accumulate heavy energies that are not beneficial. They become dull and lose power. As you work with them, you can feel when they need to be cleared. Clear them before and after any healing work and energize them when they feel dull.

You can clear your sacred tools by cleansing them with sage or tobacco smoke before and after use. You can also leave them in a bowl of salt (without water) overnight or cleanse and energize them with sound instruments. To energize them, place them in the sun or use palo santo.

Keep them stored in a safe space, on your altar, or in a medicine bag. Use them with intention and always give thanks for the assistance they give you.

Interact with them as living beings; you can even give them a name if you like. Always treat your sacred objects with respect.

Animal Totems

The animal kingdom is one of the most accessible parts of nature. Even in the busiest cities, you are likely to see a robin, an ant, a dog, or a mouse. We easily identify with terrestrial animals, birds, fish, and insects because they are all around us.

Animals also have a great deal to teach us. The way these creatures have evolved over time, and their habits, skills, and feats of adaptation, can show us how to best integrate these abilities into our own lives. The shamans knew that animals, being a part of nature, are inextricably linked to us. What they saw, however, was beyond form and commercial or mechanical uses, such as for the production of food or labor. Animals, just like all parts of nature, are sacred and help us connect to the spirit world. The shamans saw each four-legged, winged, or finned creature as a divine teacher that was not separate from humans.

A totem is any symbol, object, or living thing you feel drawn to and that has significance in your life. It has meaning to you and you want to work with its energy to emulate its characteristics. Many clans, groups, or tribes may also have a particular animal totem that represents them.

Shamans closely studied and gave reverence to each animal that crossed their path, provided them with food, or taught them a valuable lesson. They often wore objects derived from animals to demonstrate their connection to a specific animal and also to embody its skills and energies. For example, a shaman may wear an animal skin or feathers to evoke the hunting power of a beast or the vision of a bird. These objects are sacred and not used as mere decoration. A jaguar tooth necklace or a feathered headdress are symbols of respect and status to indicate a shaman's direct relationship with the animal.

How Shamans Use Totems

Shamans work with totems on both physical and metaphysical levels. This means they form a bond with both the three-dimensional creature and the invisible, spiritual essence of it. These totems act as guides and helping spirits for shamans as they traverse the material and immaterial worlds. They have learned to harness the distinctive skills of an animal totem to assist them with their shamanic work. For example, a shaman may call on the energy of the jaguar or panther, a nighttime animal, when navigating the Lower World.

Through the ritual use of totems and ceremony, shamans know how to connect our conscious waking state to one that transcends the ethereal and invisible realms. Ancient medicine women and men spent centuries studying the habits of the animals to understand them better. They learned their movements, their habits, even their way of communication, which differs from those of humans. Through their observations, they understood and respected the special qualities of each individual species. They saw the miracle of birds taking flight and considered this the dominion of the soul and the Upper World. They watched the wolves hunt in packs and understood the value of teamwork. They observed the salmon swimming upriver, against the current, and they learned the importance of perseverance.

Every element of nature has a great deal to teach us, if we learn to tap into its essence and see beyond form and function. Each creature has its own individual spirit and medicine, just like you. By studying each totem carefully, you can learn to access the energy, skills, and characteristics of any animal and understand how the spiritual world is appearing and manifesting in your own life.

Ceremony: Connect with Your Animal Totem

Begin by asking a few questions about the interactions you've had with various animals during your life:

» Is there a specific animal, reptile, bird, insect, or marine creature that has always fascinated you? Which animal(s) did you love as a child?

» Do you have statues, pictures, sculptures, or jewelry of specific types of animals?

» When scrolling social media or the internet, are there certain types of animals that catch your eye, or do you like watching certain types of animal videos or films?

» Do you see a particular creature frequently when you are outside in nature?

» Have you ever been bitten, scared, or attacked by a close animal encounter? (This physical interaction is often a clue about how the animal relates to you. Animal attacks are also one way a shaman may get tested, to see if they can survive the attack.)

» Is there a specific creature that scares you? (Usually, the fear of an animal can also teach us about the things in our lives we do not wish to see.)

» Do you repeatedly dream about a particular animal?

Once you have a better idea of what types of animals interest you or you have been connected with, you can enter a meditation to meet one of your animal totems. Stay open-minded during this process. Your animal totem chooses you, not the other way around. You must be mindful not to attach certain meanings, judgments, or favoritism to your totem. Do not fixate on a specific one to help boost your ego or what you believe the animal should be based on your preferences. As long as you stay neutral and energetically open to your animal totem, the right one will present itself to you and provide guidance.

Find a quiet place where you will not be disturbed for 15 to 30 minutes. You may play some soft music in the background or use a rattle or drum for a slow, rhythmic beat.

Sitting or lying down, pay attention to your breath and spend a few minutes relaxing the body and quieting the mind. Visualize yourself in a place of nature and look for a tall tree with deep roots. Look for an opening inside the tree, where you can crawl in.

Once inside, you will feel as if you are traversing the inner parts of the tree. Follow the roots downward and feel it getting slightly darker. It may feel like you are walking down a tunnel. Continue to follow this direction, until eventually you see a small light or an opening on the other side.

Follow the light and you will find yourself on the other side of a wide field or meadow. Take a moment to absorb the sights and sounds. Sit down among the grass and the bushes. If you see another tree, feel free to sit next to it. Enjoy this new spot in nature.

As you continue slowly breathing, keep your mind clear but alert for any movement or sound. Intend for your animal totem to appear to you. It may emerge

slowly from the tall grass or just behind the tree trunk. You may only see a shadow or hear a small growl, cry, or sound.

Remember to look both above and below. When you have spotted your animal, make eye contact and look at one another with respect. Note its size, color, and shape. Ask whether this totem has a message for you; if not, simply allow it to return to beyond the meadow or the shadows. If you are not visual, you might get the feeling of the animal, or you might hear its name. Trust whatever comes up.

Return to the opening of the tree where you originally started. Walk back down along the tunnel and to your original place in nature. Thank your animal totem for showing itself to you. Over time, as you continue to build a relationship with your totem, you will learn how to direct its medicine for improving your own life.

Additional Ways to Connect to Your Animal Totem

» Do research and study your animal for its habits, abilities, and geographic location.

» Watch documentaries or films to learn more about your totem.

» Draw, sketch, or color pictures of your chosen animal. Place small figurines or images of them around your home or office.

» Any time you can observe the animal in the wild, take the effort to closely observe its color, shape, sound, and movements. Observation and attention are the highest forms of appreciation.

» Donate or volunteer to an environmental organization that helps protect your totem.

» Share stories and pictures on social media to spread awareness and education.

Power Animals Versus Spirit Animals

In many cultures, the terms *power animal*, *totem*, and *spirit animal* may be used interchangeably. However, there are subtle differences between the names, and these can also vary depending on the tradition.

A power animal typically bonds with you at the time of birth. It will serve as your guide and protector. Sometimes, it will share many similarities and characteristics with your own personality and vibration. A power animal is also a creature from which you can derive power, especially in times of stress or hardship. Their energy can help propel you forward.

A spirit animal shifts and changes over time, depending on the situation. At various times of your life, you may require a different avenue of support. This is when a specific spirit animal may be presented to work with you. This spirit animal brings attention to parts of your life that need action and exploration. They are there to help guide you on your journey and provide healing messages that connect to your spirit.

Animal totems represent your team of power animals, spirit animals, and animals that you call upon to work with. Animal totems may also appear for you as a form of divination, to send you a message. Animal totems may also be from other realms, for example, it is possible to have a unicorn as a power animal—these people always have a magickal energy to them.

When you learn the essence of either your power animal or your spirit animal, you will also able to tap into the gifts and skills of that animal. For example, if your spirit animal is a monarch butterfly, which travels nearly 3,000 miles each year to a warmer climate, then the gift it shares with you is endurance.

Generally, you may have one or two power animals you work with throughout your life, but you may receive numerous helping spirit animals at different times. The key is to consciously interact with and know all the miraculous creatures that surround you every day.

COMMON SHAMANIC ANIMAL TOTEMS

BEAR: Bears are powerful symbols of courage through adversity. With their hibernation cycle, the bear totem teaches us how to rest and rejuvenate through the winter. They are also very protective parents.

WOLF: This totem epitomizes family, loyalty, and the call of the wild. Wolf packs live in highly structured social structures and territories. They are highly intelligent and possess complex communication skills. The wolf totem can teach us how to work together and express ourselves more fully.

JAGUAR/PANTHER: A generally nocturnal animal, this sleek cat is at the top of the food chain. They move effortlessly and teach us how to conserve energy when they are not hunting. Jaguars have an extremely powerful bite. It represents fierceness and teaches us to go after what we want.

SNAKE: A very misunderstood creature, snakes are vital in the environment. They perform pest control and help maintain a balanced ecosystem. Snakes are also known for shedding their skin, which symbolizes removing what is no longer needed from your life. This totem signals rebirth and is an ancient emblem for healing. It is still used today in Western medicine as the symbol of the caduceus, or two snakes spiraling around a rod.

HUMMINGBIRD: This very tiny bird flies far distances in search of nectar. The hummingbird teaches us how to find the sweetness in every situation. They bring joy into your life and remind us to stay light and hopeful.

EAGLE: An apex predator, the eagle shows us how to soar to new heights. This bird has highly acute vision and reminds us to see the bigger picture. The ancients believed this animal was closest to the Creator because of its ability to fly up in the sky. The eagle teaches us to find our highest selves by releasing what no longer serves us and to cocreate with the universe.

14
Deeper Shamanic Practices

We are born into a society programmed to label everything as good or bad, right or wrong, light or dark. As humans, we came into an experience with the illusion of separation. The polarities—the positive and negative—are what propel us to search for growth and ascend to higher levels of consciousness. It is the contrast between light and dark that allows us to have the full experience of this universe.

When we deny the dark, the lower aspects of ourselves—the ego, the shadow, the negative thoughts and emotions—we deny a part of ourselves. We need to embrace these aspects as they show us where we need to heal. What we strive for as beings is to have balance between our light and dark aspects, which brings us into oneness, wholeness, neutrality, and unity.

The shadow self is a part of each of us. It is an aspect of ourselves that we have repressed and stored in our unconscious. When we experience impulses or qualities that we seem not identify with, or that feel uncomfortable or trigger pain, we judge ourselves and we unintentionally push those aspects of ourselves away. We fight, flee, or fear anything that

is an aspect of the shadow self. We hold on to rigid belief systems and are not open to anything new. We attach ourselves to ideals that don't really serve our inner being.

Shadow work is a way of becoming conscious of what is unconscious in you—it is bringing the light into the darkness to achieve alchemy. You learn not to blame anything outside of you for your life, knowing the people and situations in your life are always mirrors for you that are serving your remembering. You are able to observe yourself and open up to compassion and forgiveness, which will open up your heart chakra to unconditional love and divine alignment.

When you take 100 percent responsibility for

your thoughts, emotions, actions, words, relationships, and life experiences, you are able to release what no longer serves you. Allowing you to reclaim parts of you that were hidden and not accessible before. Shadow work, cord cutting, and shamanic journeying are ways you can call fragmented parts of yourself back home to you. You are accepting, loving, and bringing back disowned parts of yourself—returning your lost soul pieces back to you. By speaking decrees and prayers you are stating your intentions and aligning to your self-sovereign power. These practices assist you through shamanic initiations on your journey of connecting to your soul.

Shadow Work

We all have shadow aspects, and the shadow self has many sides to it. It is the part of you that brings up so much fear around change and trying something new that you never start, or that you start but don't finish. It is the part of you that seeks attention and recognition for selfish reasons, or the part of you that dims your light and is afraid to shine. The shadow keeps us in a continuous loop of self-sabotage. We judge ourselves internally in the same way: we bind ourselves with shame and guilt about not being good enough, being too much, or not being what we think others expect of us.

The shadow self is the overcritical part of you that blames and judges yourself and others. When we hold judgments on other people, we are not allowing their view to be as it is, we are not allowing them to be as they are, on their unique journey and we reject them. Whatever your deepest triggers are, the ones that create resistance in you, the things that bother you about others, the things you judge about others—the triggers that anger you, repulse you, frustrate you, and overtake your sense of inner peace—are the unhealed aspects that you reject as being a part of you. As has been said, "What we resist, persists." For example, when we don't do the inner work on jealousy, it will tend to come up again and again.

We push these things away because, at some point, we had wound or trauma around them. It could be sexual abuse, manipulation, a car accident, or feeling unloved as a child—as a coping mechanism, we disown the emotions brought on from the trauma and repress them into the unconscious. This is why our culture has so much fear, guilt, and shame. The trauma causes us to be fearful and we have underlying guilt for events that occurred in the past. We have shame because we are ashamed of these parts of ourselves that we repress.

When you engage in shadow work, you can use your triggers as tools and access points to uncover the deeper meanings behind why they bother you. When something triggers you, you are being shown a shadow aspect of yourself. You observe your reactions and thoughts; you sit with the feelings as a neutral, compassionate witness and ask yourself questions, such as:

» What triggers you about this situation?
» Do you have unresolved healing around this issue?
» What are you repressing around this trigger?
» Can you accept that this aspect is also within you?
» What can you learn from this?
» What can you let go of?

When you begin shadow work, you may not realize

you were acting from a trigger until you have already responded to it. When we are in the emotional response of being triggered by some situation, we often snap back, say mean things, deny, and project by blaming the other person's behavior. This is a call for help from our wounded inner child that needs healing. Recognize the patterns in how you react and behave. Practice stepping back and observing yourself when triggered, and then go within and do shadow work. Acknowledge and honor all the aspects that are within you. By doing this, you can transmute and integrate the charged energy into neutral.

Everything in your reality is always a mirror for you—reflecting back what is in you and showing you what you need to see about yourself. This mirror shows you the parts that need to be loved and acknowledged. When you know your inner self, you will be able to stop judging and projecting. When you come into stillness and neutrality around something that has an emotional charge, you can heal the trauma within yourself. Reclaim your self-love and have compassion for yourself and others. The vibration of love and gratitude has immense power to heal and shift you and ultimately shift the world around you.

Bringing in the Light

Your shadow may be hiding your greatest gifts and positive traits: your ability to inspire others, your creativity, your healing gifts, your leadership skills, your skill in communication, your unique medicine. When you start to access the wisdom underneath the pain and shadows that reside within you, the light begins to shine. Your wounds can become your greatest medicine. To know your inner self, you compassionately go within and witness all aspects of yourself. This can bring you into a place of alignment and authenticity where you truly know the core of

who you are and nothing external can throw you off center from your purpose. You begin to amplify your inner light out to the world.

When we allow someone to be themselves, it doesn't mean that we agree and that it aligns with our personal truth. We need not attack them or shame them. We can even still like certain aspects of them and like them. We need not label or judge anything; we allow them to be who they are. We live in diversity and we are not meant to be all the same. Practicing neutrality is allowing others to have their own views and experiences without reaction or judgment. Observing from a place of stillness within will free up mental and emotional energy. Embodiment of neutrality and energetic balance is freedom and gives you access to your deepest knowing, clarity, answers and Higher Self. When we are in our center, we can witness and love all aspects of ourselves and others, that is true transformation of the shadow into light and true liberation. We move from separation to unity consciousness.

When you sit in ceremony and prayer, when you are in meditation, when you are in nature, you can ask for guidance around what you want to learn about your shadow self. You assess where you are projecting onto others. You can witness, recognize, and release those wounds and traumas; you release the stories you tell yourself; you release what is no longer serving you; and you release the timelines where the wound was created or where the programming took place. Practice calling all your energy back into your auric field—visualize, feel, and know that your energy is returning to you. Feel your energy body as solid and impenetrable—know that you are whole and perfect.

When you acknowledge all parts of yourself with compassion and love, you call forth healing into your aura and soul. This is a way you can retrieve

soul pieces. When these soul parts come back to you, you want to integrate them, and you do that by witnessing them and honoring them, letting them be a part of you. When you retrieve your soul pieces and lost fragments of yourself (the unconscious, rejected parts of you), your energy bodies activate and your vibration raises, you come into deeper alignment with your inner self and spirit.

Prayers and Decrees

Prayers, invocations, and decrees are another way to transmute ego, wounds, traumas, shadow, and bring in the light—aligning you with your divine essence and highest expression. By commanding out loud what you intend, you are able to clear and shift energies. When you call forth higher energies by speaking your intentions, you activate your energy field and DNA. By stating and embodying your intentions you begin to connect to higher frequencies and levels of consciousness.

Preparing to State Your Decree

A vital aspect when saying the words is that you are in your heart coherence (see page 60). When you are coherent, you can truly feel, and you are aligned with your higher power. Through sincerely feeling with a positive emotion we can create our reality. When repeating the decree, if you feel sad, afraid, angry, or any feelings that come up, feel them and then bring them into neutral. If you feel any energetic cords between you and the person you can cut them (see page 61). When you feel complete, scan your body and determine if any lower emotions need to be transmuted. You should feel lighter and calm.

Continue to recite the words until you can bring in forgiveness, gratitude, and love.

Reflect on the person, situation, or trait that you want to shift. These words, expressed from the heart, allow for the clearing of the energies around it and for transformation to happen.

Do not worry whether you're doing it "right"—these are suggestions, you can come up with your own words that resonate with you. Focus on the person, wound, trauma, situation, energy you want to call forth, virtually anything, and say the words.

Clearing Relationships

_____ (Other person's name)

I release any resentments and judgements towards you across all lifetimes

I ask for healing and I forgive myself and I forgive you

I declare that we are in harmony with each other, I love you

Thank you, and so it is, Aho

Clearing Your Shadow Aspects

_____ (Self-sabotage)

I no longer need you as a protective mechanism

I release the wounding that caused me to feel undeserving

I bring light and healing into this aspect of myself

I now align with my Higher Self

Thank you, and so it is, Aho

Aligning to Your Higher Self

_____ (I call forth the highest levels of light into my being)

I am in alignment with my inner divinity and Higher Self

I am sovereign and guided by the truth of my soul's purpose

I declare that I am in service to my Highest Source. Thank you, and so it is, Aho

When you say your decrees, know that you have shifted and created change. The areas you can affect are endless (e.g. ancestral traumas, past-life healing, karma, emotional issues, fears, illness), and you can clear across all lifetimes, which will align you with your highest timeline. If something new comes up for you, you have the tools to heal yourself. It is magickal to watch the benefits unfold in your life, from the feelings of unity and being connected to all things, to having an open heart and the ability to create and manifest your dreams. Your relationships shift. There is ease and joy in your life. Stating your prayers and decrees as a daily practice is a way to empower yourself. By bringing in more spiritual light into your world you can connect to your higher purpose.

Shamanic Divination

We are interconnected to everything and the world around us. Shamanic divination is a way to communicate with the spirit world by gaining answers, guidance, and information. Divination can be done by journeying to the spirit world and it can also be done in the Middle World through our interactions with everything around us, from animals and plants to nature spirits, numbers, and signs.

The Divine is always offering us communication in ways we can decode. Through signs, symbols, synchronicity, dreams, metaphors, numbers, and mirrors, the world can guide us, teach us, and help us

heal ourselves. The more present and aware you are in your day-to-day life, and when you are aligned with heart-brain coherence, the more you can tap into your truth and receive your answers.

The conscious mind is logical and analytical, and the subconscious mind doesn't know the difference between fantasy and reality. That is why the subconscious responds so well to ceremony and why ceremony is so powerful for our psyche. Spirits will communicate with us in various abstract and symbolic ways, depending on what we are open to receiving. Once you pay attention, you will learn to understand the messages and synchronicities. Our entire world can become an oracle.

Shamanic Oracle Walk Practice

Determine your intention or question. Put your question out into the universe and ask for signs on your walk. Go on a walk and pay attention to everything that appears for you—any animals, signs, numbers on cars or homes, or sounds you hear. Be present to anything that gives you an intuitive nudge. Once you set your intention, anything that comes into your field of awareness can give you information and guidance. Focus your awareness on your breath and stay fully present to what comes your way. It might be a bird, symbol, or number. Sometimes a license plate will give you a sequence of numbers or words that you know intuitively is guidance. If you see something, such as an animal or numbers, you go within to find what the message is for you or you can look up the symbolism (there are plenty of books or websites on numerology and animal symbolism). Be patient, as it can take practice. You will begin to get you in touch with the interconnectedness of all things.

Butterfly Medicine

Everything is alive, everything has a spirit; therefore, everything is sacred. It is how you hold this sacredness within yourself and your everyday life that you engage in the practice of shamanism and bring healing. This worldview can bring you much comfort. When you know you are not alone, when you know you have a higher purpose, and when you know you are a vital part of this Earth, you have a sense of purpose and grounding.

In my first year of formal shamanic studies, we went on a shamanic journey to retrieve a spirit animal that would assist us with our healing. In my journey, a caterpillar is what came—a caterpillar. While still in the journey, I tried to reject the caterpillar. I wanted an animal and not a bug. And I wanted something more prestigious. I even rejected the caterpillar by questioning why I wasn't getting another animal that I felt was supposed to come. The caterpillar did not waiver and no animal came to replace it.

Every time I receive a new animal totem (see page 67) in my life, there is always a message for me. It always has some medicine for me. Especially when it appears at the perfect time to bring me clarity or when it is so random as to jar me and get my attention about something. And so I researched the caterpillar, and I spent time delving into and understanding the caterpillar's process.

A caterpillar does not consciously know the journey that lies ahead. When it consumes enough energy, it builds a chrysalis: it sheds its outer layer of skin, and the chrysalis hardens, forming a tough outer shell. Inside, the caterpillar goes through metamorphosis and eventually emerges. The caterpillar is not even conscious of the process it is going through. As a butterfly, it spreads its wings and flies freely into a completely new life—a life it could have never imagined before.

When we consider a caterpillar's journey to become a butterfly—the metamorphosis and transformation that comes after the initiation—it teaches us so much about life. When we engage in shamanic work, we experience this process repeatedly, as our old structures and ways of being are shed and we eventually emerge into a new life.

I realized that the caterpillar had so much to teach me about the journey I was on. Like many people, I was healing from intense traumas and I had huge fears about trusting people and trusting myself. The medicine of this fuzzy insect was showing me that the reality I was in was not my destiny—and that I would go through a process of transformation and rebirth. The caterpillar was a guide for me to go within, let go of the past, and shed my skin when it was no longer serving me.

The caterpillar accepts the changes and trusts in the journey. This experience holds so much power and symbolism for me because as I continued on my journey, caterpillars would always show up during significant moments, during life changes, and during my shamanic initiations.

The caterpillar stage is the shadow work, the Lower World of the unconscious, and the shamanic initiation.

The butterfly teaches us to have full faith in the journey and the changes in our body and life. It shows us how to live in the present moment with joy and lightness of being. The butterfly doesn't fear change, and it doesn't worry about the past or the future. It is a symbol of the soul and the connection shared by all things.

The medicine the caterpillar brought me allowed me to soften a little more, to trust my process. It helped me know it was okay not to know how things would unfold. And I reminded myself that eventually I would spread my wings and fly into a bright new world.

"Perhaps the butterfly is proof that you can go through a great deal of darkness yet become something beautiful."

—Unknown

References

Chapter 2

Markowski, George. "Information Theory." *Encyclopedia Britannica*. https://www.britannica.com/science/information-theory/Physiology#:~:text=In%20other%20words%2C%20the%20human,only%2050%20bits%20per%20second.

Chapter 3

"Quick Coherence® Technique." HeartMath is a registered trademark of Quantum Intech, Inc. For all HeartMath trademarks, go to www.heartmath.com/trademarks.

Chapter 4

Inlak'ech, Diana Quinn. "Why Ancestral Healing?" June 14, 2017. 2www.drdianaquinn.com/blog/j5emle8xzbc5y6jxcezx66cxhxnda7.

Kagey, Emily. "'Junk DNA' Isn't So Useless After all." April 11, 2018. www.futurity.org/junk-dna-1728712.

Chapter 13

Kingston, Karen. *Creating Sacred Space with Feng Shui*. New York: Broadway Books, 1997.

Acknowledgments

It has been an honor and a privilege to write this book. I am thankful to all the souls who have crossed my path—each and every person who has been a part of my journey has had something to teach me and has contributed to my growth.

I would like to give a heartfelt thank you to my brothers, Corey and Adam, and to my Dad, Tim, who were unable to heal from addiction in this life. They have been my greatest teachers and helpers from the other side.

I am grateful to Johnny for all his love and support and for being my rock. I thank my entire family for their unconditional love—my sister, Amanda, for being a wise friend and mirror; my brother, Zack, for his resilience; and my Mom, Laurel, for her pure heart and laughter. I would also like to thank my Yorkie, Zeus, for his playful spirit and my cousin, Melanie, for being such a cheerleader in my life.

I would not be able to do what I do without the love and support of the Shaman Sisters community. I have always been grateful to have a platform that allowed me to reach people all over the world. Whether for an online order, an in-store customer, a ceremony, a course, or a treatment session—I am deeply humbled for the opportunity that you give me to be of service. This book would not have been created without you and I can't thank you enough for your trust.

I have immense gratitude for Jill Alexander for believing in me and in shamanism, and for offering your wisdom and literally making my dream of writing this book a reality.

I would like to thank the entire team at Fair Winds Press for making this process a delight. Thank you, Jenna Patton, for your brilliance and for guiding me in the process; Karen Levy, for your organization; Nyle Vialet, for being so open and bringing everything together; Heather Godin, for your artistry; and Lydia Anderson, for your advice and for helping to get the book out to the world. I would also like to thank the design team and everyone one else at The Quarto Group who had a role in making this book possible. I have great appreciation for all the work and collaboration that went into this creation.

Roberta Orpwood helped to make this book something special with her magnificent creativity and transmissions that can be felt through her work. I am so thankful and blessed for the synchronicity of having her as the illustrator. I am grateful to Nikolina Zelic for capturing the gorgeous images—I really enjoyed creating them with you!

I am deeply thankful to the Shaman Sisters team: Your passion to create a positive change and healing in the world is inspiring. From our intentional jewelers who handcraft everything we make with love to our customer service team who take pride in their work and truly care. Thank you! I am so incredibly honored to be surrounded by a team who strives to embody unity consciousness, have high standards, and love what they do—Tiffany, Jen, Vanessa, and Eva. Thank you, Sisters, for everything you bring to our community. I would like to give a special thanks to Alice for all your support and ideas. Tiffany for your creativity. Thank you, Alexa, for being a part of the Shaman Sisters team and for your gorgeous images. Schara, thank you for your magic.

I know that when women step into their power, they give other women the inspiration to do the same. When women genuinely celebrate one another's successes, they release generations of programming—sisterhood is sacred. Having strong women in my life who see me, hold space for me, love me, and honor me has been such a gift. To my incredible Soul Sisters: Francie, Katica, Amanda, Kelly, Amber, Jacqui, Alice, Melanie, Carly, Stacy, and my Birth Sister, Amanda—thank you for being on this journey with me. I love you.

To the masters and teachers who have guided my path, including Janet, Gael, Marylin, Mario, Ginny, Andrew, Arianna, and Alice: Your presence has helped me to heal and has shaped who I am. I have so much respect, love, and gratitude for you. Thank you to the Great Spirit and to my Higher Self for one of the most beautiful initiations of my life.

Thank you to my ancestors for your assistance and presence from the other world. Thank you to the guardians for your love and protection. I am grateful to the plant spirits, the animals, and the natural world for your teachings and synchronicities.

I would like to acknowledge the beautiful Indigenous Peoples, First Nations Peoples, and the Tribes. I honor you and thank you for sharing your sacred wisdom and teachings. Some of the proceeds from this book will be donated to Indigenous communities.

Thank you, I honor you, I love you, A'ho.

About the Author

Rebecca Keating is the creator of Shaman Sisters®, a global website distinguished for offering high quality crystals, gemstone jewelry, and other sacred tools. She holds a bachelor of science in nursing and also worked as a registered nurse in many areas, including teaching other nurses and being a director of care prior to founding Shaman Sisters.

Rebecca has immersed herself in shamanic studies from numerous traditions, including Celtic, Andean, Toltec, and Incan shamanism, and she is a mesa carrier in the Q'ero tradition. She has trained with teachers from around the world and under Indigenous healers and Shamans in South America.

Rebecca is a Shamanic Practitioner, Energy and Crystal Healer, HeartMath Interventions Practitioner, Ecstatic Dance Facilitator, Sound Healing Practitioner, and Kambo Practitioner.

Shaman Sisters' crystal boutique is located in Port Credit, Canada, and is also the physical home to The Aura Room, a sacred space where Rebecca offers her private healing practice. The space is a hub for community events, trainings and workshops, shamanic ceremonies, and virtual offerings.

Rebecca honors the interconnectedness of all things and has deep reverence for the Earth and all of her creatures: the plants, animals, elementals, and humans. She is an avid supporter of local and international marginalized groups, tribes, and Indigenous initiatives and Indigenous artists. She is passionate about being of service and guiding others to connect to their inner Source and to realize their gifts and fullest potential.

Shaman Sisters is a movement uniting community from all parts of the world. Together we can raise the frequency of the planet. Stay connected @shamansisters.

About the Illustrator

Roberta Orpwood is a Professional Visionary Artist, Reiki Master Teacher, and Shamanic Sound and Energy Healer who works from her private Studio and Therapy Practice within South West London.

Her delicate watercolor paintings are influenced by her love of natural beauty, the female figure, the spirit of nature, and the mystery of the human soul. Her creations are predominantly figurative, expressing beauty beyond the limits of the physical body. They represent a divine feminine that resides within all of us, and her compositions are often inspired by the visions she receives during her shamanic journeying and meditation practice. They include not only goddesses but spirit animals, guides, elementals, and soul portraits, with themes of love, healing, and empowerment.

www.soulbirdart.com

Index